Unleashing the Trends in Contemporary Management Issues

Advisory Committee

Prof. Subhansu Bandyopadhyay: Former Professor, Computer Science & Engg., University of Calcutta & Ex-Vice Chancellor of Brainware University, India

Prof. M. N. Bandyopadhyay: Director, Haldia Institute of Technology & Ex-Director NIT Kurukshetra, India

Shri. Rahul Bose: Global Manager, Learning & Knowledge, IBM Global Business Services and Co-Chairperson, Bengal Chamber of Commerce & Industry, West Bengal, India

Prof. Debasish Sur: Department of Commerce, The University of Burdwan, West Bengal, India

Prof. Mrinalini Pandey : Department of Management Studies, IIT-ISM, Dhanbad, India

Prof. Gautam Bandhopadhyay: Department of Management Studies, NIT, Durgapur, India

Editors

Adrinil Santra: Assistant Professor, School of Management & Social Sciences, Haldia Institute of Technology

Manigrib Bag: Assistant Professor, School of Management & Social Sciences, Haldia Institute of Technology

Dr. Arunangshu Giri: Associate Professor, School of Management & Social Sciences, Haldia Institute of Technology

Dr. Anjan Mishra: Registrar, Haldia Institute of Technology

Unleashing the Trends in Contemporary Management Issues

Editors

Adrinil Santra

Manigrib Bag

Dr. Arunangshu Giri

Dr. Anjan Mishra

ABHIJEET PUBLICATIONS

NEW DELHI 110002

ABHIJEET PUBLICATIONS
4658-A, First Floor, Ambika Bhawan,
21 Ansari Road, New Delhi 110002
Phone: 011-23259444
E-mail: abhijeetpublication@gmail.com
www.abhijeetpublications.com

UNLEASHING THE TRENDS IN CONTEMPORARY MANAGEMENT ISSUES

First Published 2020

ISBN 978-93-88865-33-3

PRINTED IN INDIA

Published by J.K. Singh for Abhijeet Publications, New Delhi-110002, Lasertypeset by Abhijeet Typesetters, New Delhi and Printed at Dynamic Printers, New Delhi.

From the Editors' Desk

The world history of business has traversed a route of Raw material economy, Product economy, Service economy and experiential economy successively. India is no exception. During the recent times there has been an indication of volatility and uncertainty in the Country's economy. The managerial jobs have become stressed which has further deteriorated by excessive competition and existence of many players in every niche of the market. Research workers have initiated divergence in focus to address different domains to identify their effects on management styles and achievement. The prominent stakeholders in the scene namely the consumer market, society and Government have increased complexity in the state of affairs.

After a long run in the post liberalization era Indian economy in now driven by consumerism and market which are again subject to many forces involving every socioeconomic parameters and international framework under different regulatory and funding bodies. It is the high time to have in depth study to curve out the right strategy for inclusive growth with sustainability. This volume has considered different contemporary issues attached with management research from valued research workers only to cater the need of the formulators of better strategy and sensitize the researchers' community to probe into different domains of importance with a focus on corpo-social substrate of India.

The issues of women empowerment, healthcare capital, inventory control, literacy status, social crime, retail activities, study of human capital etc which are of immense importance and already created demand of thought in the research arena are palpably covered. The issues like women harassment in workplace, digitization of employment are of utmost importance so far as inclusive growth is concerned. The papers on cloud based technology, search engine optimization etc. have tried to cover a proper subset of techno management area. Service based industries like tourism and retail having high level of importance in the growth of Indian economy have attracted many research workers to go in depth which, we, have considered for selection.

Overall in this volume we the editors have tried to cover divergent topics which are directly influencing the economy as a whole. If this proves to be helpful for the readers for their knowledge thirst, strategy formulation, research in the management domain and help to know our country in a better way then our endeavour will be successful.

We the editors will be thankful if you all go through these papers thoroughly and revert us the feedback for continuous development. We also express our heartfelt gratitude to our valued contributors for their honest and untiring efforts.

With ardent expectation of constructive feedback from the readers' side,

Yours faithfully,

Adrinil Santra
Manigrib Bag
Dr. Arunangshu Giri
Dr. Anjan Mishra

Contents

List of Contributors

1. Dr. Debasish Biswas: Assistant Professor, Dept. of Business Administration, Vidyasagar University, West Bengal.
2. Dr. Kaushik Kundu: Associate Professor, Dept. of Management & Business Administration, Aliah University, West Bengal

   Dr. Dev Narayan Sarkar: Associate Director, PepsiCo India, West Bengal.
3. Dr. Pradip Paul: Senior Manager, Haldia Divisional Office, Indian Oil Corporation Ltd., Haldia, West Bengal.
4. Dr. Santanu Ray Chaudhuri: Assistant Professor, The Neotia University, West Bengal.
5. Dr. Nirmal Chandra Roy: Assistant Professor, Department of Business Administration (Human Resource), The University of Burdwan, West Bengal.
6. Sandeep Kumar & Vishnupriya: Students,Electrical Engineering Dept., Haldia Institute of Technology, West Bengal

   Dr. Dilip Dey: Professor, Electrical Engineering Dept., Haldia Institute of Technology, West Bengal
7. Dr. Soma Mishra: Assistant Professor & Deputy Controller of Examinations, Haldia Institute of Technology, West Bengal.
8. Ipsita Paria: Deputy Manager, H.D.F.C Bank Limited, West Bengal.
9. Dr. Mustak Ahmed: Assistant Professor, IMS Centre for Research, West Bengal.
10. Dola Sarkar: Assistant Professor, Budge Budge Institute of Technology, West Bengal

    Dr. Jadab Kr. Das: Associate Professor, Department of Commerce, University of Calcutta, West Bengal.

11. Dr. Sourav Gangopadhyay: Assistant Professor, Haldia Institute of Management, West Bengal

Dr. Jayeeta Majumder: Assistant Professor, Haldia Institute of Management, West Bengal.

12. Dr. Shamba Chatterjee: Assistant Professor, Department of Biotechnology, Haldia Institute of Technology, West Bengal.

13. Dr. Niladri Chakraborty: Assistant Professor, Department of Food Technology, Haldia Institute of Technology, West Bengal.

14. Satakshi Chatterjee: Assistant Professor, Haldia Institute of Management, West Bengal.

15. Dr. Jayeeta Majumder: Assistant Professor, Haldia Institute of Management, West Bengal.

Dr. Sourav Gangopadhyay: Assistant Professor, Haldia Institute of Management, West Bengal.

16. Asmita Basu: Assistant Professor, Army Institute of Management, West Bengal.

17. Jyoti Kumari Pandit: Assistant Professor, Haldia Institute of Management, West Bengal.

18. Smita Chakraborty: Assistant Professor, Haldia Institute of Health Sciences, West Bengal.

19. Abanti Aich, Assistant Professor: Hospital Management Department, Haldia Institute of Health Sciences, West Bengal.

20. Swatee Biswas: Admission Officer, Haldia Institute of Management, West Bengal.

21. Manali Basu: Assistant Professor, Golden Regency Institute of Hospitality Management, West Bengal.

1

Sexual Harassment of Women at Workplace: An Overview

Dr. Debasish Biswas

ABSTRACT

Sexual harassment of women at workplace has become an intolerable and uncontrollable menace. Among many types of exploitation against women, sexual exploitation has been the most heinous and our Hon'ble Supreme Court has stated, "Each incident of sexual harassment at the workplaceresults in violation of the fundamental right to gender equality and the right to life and liberty – the two most precious fundamental rights". Amidst various other developments, controversies and delays, the Indian legislature finally enacted the Sexual Harassment of Women at Workplace (Prevention, Prohibition and Redressal) Act,2013 (Act No.14 of 2013), with an objective to protect women against sexual harassment at workplace and to put in place a redressal mechanism to handle complaints. It was in fact in this case for the very first time, that sexual harassment at the workplace was acknowledged to be a human rights violation. The act has effectively adopted and revised the guidelines laid down in the Vishakajudgment with added provision of rigor and compliance. The paper takes up the issue in both theoretical as well as practical way. It begins with defining the concept of sexual harassment and then looks into the various theories explaining the reasons for the occurrence of these issues. Then the paper looks at the after effects of the Vishaka case as well as the preventive measures related to the above mentioned Act. It also identifies certain loopholes in the provisions of the said legislation.

Key Words: prevention, redressal, sexual harassment, vishakajudgment, women, workplace.

Introduction

On 9th December, 2013 "The Sexual Harassment of Women at Workplace (Prevention,Prohibition and Redressal) Act 2013" has come into force. The Act is based on the Supreme Court guidelines in the case of Vishaka vs. State of Rajasthan [1997 JT (7) 384]. During the 90s, the most controversial and brutal gangrape at the workplace involved, Bhanwari Debi, a Rajasthan state government employee who tried to prevent child marriage as part of her duties as a social worker of the Women Development Programme. The feudal patriarchs who were enraged by her (in their words: a lowly women from a poor and potter community) 'guts' decided to teach her a lesson and raped her repeatedly. Vishaka guidelines, as laid down by theSupreme Court put the onus of a safe working environment on the employer. The guidelines also state that it shall be the duty of the employer or other responsible persons in work places or other institutions to prevent or deter the commission of acts of sexual harassment and to provide the procedures for the resolution, settlement or redressal of acts of sexual harassment by taking all steps required. The guidelines also lay down a grievance redressal mechanism that mandates all companies, whether operating in the public or private sector, to set up Complaints Committee within the organisation to look into such offences.

Objectives of the Study

This study would explore the problems of working women regarding sexual harassment at their workplaces. Making the study more penetrating, the focus has been given not only to the types of sexual harassment, but also to the preventive measures related to it. The prime objectives of the study are:

1. To make a clear concept of harassment and sexual harassment;
2. To identify and explain different theories regarding sexual harassment;
3. To study the extent and nature of sexual harassment;
4. To find out the strategies for preventing sexual harassment;
5. To discuss the penalties regarding sexual harassment; and
6. To criticise 'The Sexual Harassment of Women at Workplace (Prevention, Prohibition and Redressal) Act 2013'.

Methodology

The study is primarily descriptive in nature. It is based on analytical method to understand the nature of sexual harassment, the role of the state to protect the rights of the working women, and above all, the remedies to prevent such issues. For this study, secondary sources have beenused and examined. The findings of other scholarly studies on the same problem have also been taken into account. Different journals and the newspapers have been considered as sources of data.

Discussion and Analysis

Harassment is the application of aggressive pressure or intimidation. It covers wide range of behaviours of offensive nature and characteristically it is repetitive.

Types of Harassment:

1. Workplace harassment
2. Psychological harassment
3. Racial harassment
4. Religious harassment
5. Sexual harassment

"Sexual Harassment" includes any one or more of the following unwelcome Acts or behaviours (whether directly or by implication) namely –

1. physical contact and advances; or
2. demand or request for sexual favours; or
3. making sexually coloured remarks; or
4. showing pornography, or
5. any other unwelcome physical, verbal or non-verbal conduct of sexual nature.

Definition of Sexual Harassment:

Sexual harassment is a form of sex discrimination composed of two forms of behaviour: quid pro quo harassment and hostile environment harassment. Quid pro quo harassment involves sexual threats or bribery that are made a condition of employment or used as the basis for employment decisions. Hostile environment harassment captures those behaviours, such as sexual jokes, comments and touching, that interfere with an individual's ability to do her/his job or that create an 'intimidating, hostile or offensive working environment'.Catharine Mackinnon (1979) defines sexual harassment as 'an unwanted imposition of sexual requirements in the context of relationship of unequal power' **(1).** Likewise, Kathleen Gallivan (1991) defines sexual harassment as 'any type of unwanted sexual or gender oriented behaviourthat has adverse job-related effects'. Ultimately, sexual harassment is often about letting women know they are not welcome in certain workplaces and that they are not respected members of the work group. Sexual harassment continues to happen employment opportunities for many women and men.

Historical Perspective

Sexual harassment was first documented in 1908(**2**). It was recognised and labelled as problem and the first research in the area emerged during 1970s(**3**). Sexual harassment is considered both a legal as well as a psychological phenomenon (**4**). Documenting the prevalence of sexual harassment has been one of the first research efforts made in the area(**5**).

Theories on Sexual Harassment: There are various theories as to why sexual harassment happens. We will look into these theories for our general understanding.

1. Natural /Biological Model: This model proposes sexual harassment is the natural outcome of men's stronger sex drive and men's role as the sexual aggressor**(6).**

2. The Socio-cultural model: This model proposes that sexual harassment is a product of culturally legitimated power and status differences between men and women**(7).** Sexual harassment is perceived to be an outgrowth of the gender socialization process and is a mechanism by which men assert power and dominance over women both at work and in society**(8).** This model also emphasizes how individual- level correlates, such as age and marital status, mediate women's low status and lack of socio-cultural power. For example, single and young women may be viewed as more available for sexual interaction than do other women, and hence, they may experience higher levels of sexual harassment than other women. Some argue that age not only captures the 'impact of youth per se' but is also a proxy for low seniority or poor job status**(9).**

3. Formal and Informal Organization Power: Individuals with formal organizational power, such as managers, may use their position to harass subordinates. Organizational power must be broadened to include interpersonal modes of power. For example, co-workers with individual or informal sources of power, such as personality, expertise and access to critical information, may be more likely to engage in harassment than others**(10)**.

4. Numerical and Normative Dominance: Numerically skewed sex ratios in work situations, such as female-dominated and male-dominated work groups, play a prominent role in explanations of sexual harassment. Sex role spill over theory is considered one of the primary theories of sexual harassment. For example, women in male-typed jobs are more likely to experience sexual harassment than women in female-typed and integrated occupations**(11)**.

5. The Contact Hypothesis and Numerical Dominance: The contact hypothesis (**12**) views harassment as a function of the contact between men and women in the workplace, rather than emphasizing the gender role expectations associated with certain jobs. Here, numerical dominance is seen as distinct from, though interrelated to, normative dominance. For example, a female secretary who works in an environment numerically dominated by males and who has more contact with men will experience more severe harassment than her counterparts in integrated work-places or those numerically dominated by females(**13**).

6. The Feminist Theory: With theemergence of theWomen's movement in the 60s and 70s people began to tell of their experiences of sexual assault and so a more accurate identification of the problem became possible. This approach is a sociological analysis which over the past three decades has focused on two important and previously largely ignored aspects of sexual assault-

a)The unequal power relationships between men and women and adults and children.

b)The abuser responsibility for initiating and/or maintaining sexual assault.

This approach argues that the most adequate explanation of the motivation for, and incidence of, sexual assault is found in the complex interplay between existing social structures, conventional attitudes and the differential gender socialisation of males and females in patriarchal society. It does not focus exclusively on incestuous abuse within the family; rather it is able to broaden its focus to include the dynamics of extra-familial as well as intra-familial sexual and incestuous abuse, all of which rely on males exerting their sexual power over women. It shows that sexual assault is an extension of the current legal, social, economic and political systems in which we live which manifest and reinforce male dominance over female. Unequal power relationships between men and women are embedded in social organization like, in the areas of education, employment, health, income, security, law and decision-making, women come out second best**(14)**.

7. Psychological Theory: It focuses on the abuses rather than the victim or the family. Their attentions are on:

a) Identifying a personality profile of sex offenders.

b) On isolating the motivations of abusers.

In terms of motivations for abuse, a common finding has been that alcohol or alcoholism contributes to a reduction in internal inhibitions to sex offences. Poor impulse control is also seen as a common problem. Abusers have also been found to be highly adept at rationalisation and displacing responsibility and blame onto others rather than the self. It has become clear that abusers come from all social backgrounds and are not confined to socially or economically deprived families. In addition, they do not suffer from any mental illnesses nor do they necessarily have other criminal tendencies. In fact, the sex offender is often an otherwise law-abiding 'guy next door' type**(15)**.

8. The Victim Precipitation Theory: This approach considers offenders and victims as mutually interacting partners where the victim, through signs, eye contact, gestures and words, or by being present at certain venues or being out alone sometimes encourages rape. Things like accepting a ride home, responding in a friendly manner in conversation, accepting a dinner invitation, visiting a male friend at home or inviting a male friend into her home may be misread or intentionally rationalized by the perpetrator as a sign of consent to sexual intercourse. In other words, a woman is raped because she failed to accurately communicate her desire not to have sex**(16)**. Some countries have criminalized sexual harassment in the workplace or have legislation that is considered to apply to workplace harassment. Criminal cases usually require a higher standard of proof than civil cases. In addition, women may be unwilling to report harassment when it is made a criminal offense, because although they want the harassment to stop, they do not want to subject the harasser to criminal prosecution. Finally, criminalizing sexual harassment may limit a victim's ability to recover damages, because an employer usually will not be liable for an employee's criminal conduct.

9. Psychoanalytic Theory: Freud was the first to postulate that the trauma of childhood sexual abuse resulted in later psychic damage. This was the basis of his 'seduction' theory which he presented along with detailed case studies at a major forum in 1896. The idea that fathers were sexually abusing their daughters caused such an outrage in conservative 19th century Vienna that Freud was ridiculed and shunned by his peers. In fact, Seduction Theory was so poorly received that Freud never again publicly referred to it. In 1933, in his Introductory Lectures on Psychoanalysis, he stated: "I was driven to recognise in the end that these reports (of sexual abuse) were untrue and so came to understand that the hysterical symptoms are derived from fantasies and not from real occurrences."Freud took the step of disbelieving the reports of his clients but he couldn't deny the traumatic effects or psychic damage he had observed. What he did to explain this to develop his new classic theories of psycho-sexual development in which the theoretical constructs of 'penis-envy' and the 'Oedipus Complex' are central. These theories claim that children pass through a stage of being sexually attracted to their parents (boys to their mothers and girls to their fathers). Freud argued that it is the inability to successfully resolve this psycho-sexual stage of development that gives rise to the psychic damage he observed in his clients who had reported childhood sexual abuse. The same theoretical framework also serves to explain the behaviour of offenders in 'proven' cases of sexual assault or incest. For sexual assaults the theory goes that offenders'behaviour is the result of castration anxiety as a result of the failure to resolve the Oedipus complex which gives rise to feelings of sexual inadequacy and the need to be sexually dominant. Adult sex offenders are viewed as pathologically disturbed and sexually perverted as a result of poor psycho-sexual development. The distortions in the offenders' psycho-sexual development are seen as the result of failure in his mother's parenting**(17)**. To explain incest, Freud's Oedipus complex casts the daughter as the active desiring agent who wishes her father to become her love object. The child is seen as 'seductress' while the father is seen as the passive, innocent object of his daughters' seduction: an overtly displayed invitation which he cannot help but act upon. This normalises sexual acts between parents and children by seeing them as NATURAL rather than ABUSIVE and places the responsibility clearly on the child 'victim'.Women in non-traditional jobs may be subjected to gender hazing or baiting, in the forms of sexual inquiries, jokes, remarks or innuendoes. Such behaviour has 'the effect of reminding a woman that she is viewed as object of sexual derision rather than as a credible co-worker' **(18)**.

Types of Sexual Harassment:

Gender harassment: Generalized sexist statements and behaviour that convey insulting or degrading attitudes about women. Examples include insulting remarks, offensive graffiti, obscene jokes or humour about sex or women in general.

Seductive behaviour: Unwanted, inappropriate and offensive sexual advances. Examples include repeated sexual invitation, insistent requests for dinner, drinks or dates, persistent letters, phone calls and other invitations.

Sexual bribery: Solicitation of sexual activity or other sex-linked behaviour by promise of rewards, the proposition may be either overt or subtle.

Sexual coercion: Coercion of sexual activity or other sex-linked behaviour by threat of punishment. Examples include negative performance evaluations, withholding of promotions and threat of termination.

Sexual imposition: Gross sexual imposition or sexual assault. Examples include forceful touching, feeling and grabbing.

Forms of Sexual Harassment:

1. Physical:

Touching

Unwanted massages

Patting, caressing, or fondling

Impeding or blocking movement

Standing closer than appropriate or necessary for the work being done,

Touching or rubbing oneself sexually around or in view of another person, or assault.

2. Verbal:

Sexual comments, slurs, jokes, or rumours

Verbal sexual advances, threats /propositions

Verbal abuse of a sexual nature

Making sexual comments –clothing/ body/looks

Sexually degrading words used

Suggestive/obscene letters, notes/ invitations

Turning academic discussions into sexual discussions

Asking sexual fantasies, preferences, or history

Asking questions about to social or sexual life, Insulting

3. Visual:

Leering (looking at someone in sexually suggestive manner)

Making suggestive gestures

Displaying pornography, sexually suggestive pictures, cartoons, posters or literature

Having sexually suggestive software on a work or academic computer

Suggestive or insulting sounds

Reasons why women don't complain?

Women do not report harassment for a variety of reasons ranging from a fear of retaliation or disbelief to a fear of losing one's job or making the situation even worse. Survey on working women carried out by the National Commission for Women reveals that no doubt the number of cases filed for sexual harassment has risen but women employees are still reluctant to report the matter to concerned authority. Indeed women suffer it silently and avoid lodging report because she believes that her complaint would disadvantage her in connection with her employment. They also face mental harassment caused by acts such as whistling, ogling, winking, passing of lewd remarks, reciting of obscene songs, abusing, unnecessary lambasting and sexual gestures.

Strategies for Prevention:

There are a number of steps that to reduce the risk of sexual harassment occurring in workplaces.

- **Adopt a clear sexual harassment policy**
- **Train employees**

- Train supervisors and managers
- **Monitor workplace**
- Take all complaints seriously.

Constitution of ICC: Every Employer shall, by an order in writing, constitute an Internal Complaints Committee (ICC) in all Administrative units and offices [Section 4(2)]. The Committee shall consist of:

(a) Presiding Officer (Woman at a senior level in the organization).

(b) Not less than two members from amongst the employees preferably with experience in social work orlegal knowledge.

(c) One member from NGO / persons familiar with issues of sexual harassment.

(d) 50% of total members shall be women.

Powers of ICC:ICC shall have the powers of a civil court under the Code of Civil Procedure, 1908 when trying a suit in respect of following matters;

(a) Summoning and enforcing the attendance of any person and examining him on oath;

(b) Requiring the discovery and production of documents; and

(c) Any other matter which may be prescribed.

Local Complaints Committee: Provisions are provided under the Act to form Local Complaints Committee (LCC) for every district for receiving complaints of sexual harassment from establishments where the ICC ha not been formed due to having less than 10 workers or if the complaint is against the employer himself.

Complaint Procedure: The Act stipulates that aggrieved woman can make written complaint of sexual harassment at workplace to the ICC or to the LCC (in case a complaint is against the employer), within a period of three months from the date of incident and in case of a series of incidents, within a period of three months from the date of last incident. If the aggrieved woman is unable to make complaint in writing, reasonable assistance shall be rendered by the presiding officer or any member of the ICC (or in case the aggrieved woman is unable to make complaint in writing to the LCC, the reasonable assistance shall be rendered by the Chairperson or any member of the LCC) for making the complaint in writing.

As per the Sexual Harassment of Women at Workplace (Prevention, Prohibition and Redressal) Rules, 2013**(19)**, in case the aggrieved woman is unable to make a complaint on account of her physical incapacity, a complaint may be filed inter alia by her relative or friend or her co-worker or an officer of the National Commission for Woman or State Women's Commission or any person who has knowledge of the incident, with the written consent of the aggrieved woman.

Penalties for Sexual Harassment:

When there are no Service Rules, the Committee can recommend if allegation proved to take any action which includes:

1. Written apology

Warning

Reprimand or censure

With-holding of promotion

With-holding of pay rise and increments

Termination of service

Undergoing counselling session or carrying out community service

2. For false or malicious complaint or false evidence, the Committee may recommend to take any of the above seven actions against the Complainant or any other concerned person.

3. Mere inability to prove allegation, would not attract such action.

4. By way of victim's compensation the amount is calculated in view of:

(a) sufferings

(b) medical expenses required

(c) income and financial status of the respondent

(d) feasibility in lump sum or in instalments

5. An appeal to the Appellate Authority is allowed in case of non-implementation of such recommendations.

Criticism of the Safeguards:

The Act does not cover in its scope and ambit a very important community that is agricultural workers. The exclusion of armed forces too is an inexplicable gap. Women working in the armed forces suffer highly from sexual harassment which calls for their inclusion within the purview of the Act. What needs to be noted is that the Armed Forces sector is heavily male dominated and that the chain of command is in the lair of the males. On the other hand, interestingly, various recent studies and surveys over the last few years or so have shown that very often, workplaces also involve women initiating and engaging in acts of sexual harassment. The first and most glaring flaw of this legislation is the complete absence of gender neutrality. The Act is all about sexual harassment of women and does not cater to the opposite gender. While efforts to protect women in the workplace are commendable, there appears to be no such recourse to legislative action for sexually harassed men.In an era, where the force of the law thrives for creating equal opportunity and focuses on eliminating discrimination of every kind possible, this particular Act is not at all gender neutral. The Act provides protection against acts of sexual harassment only for women and not men According to the law in place, no complaint may be filed by a male employee. There is a rising phenomenon of sexual harassment of males, which, though considerably lower than females, cannot be ignored. Although, this Act is a great step forward in protection for women, it however leaves a wide scope for false allegations. Individuals not involved in law making but who would rather be governed by this law feel, that its effect must be viewed not just on the individual in question but in totality including his family. This not only becomes a source of nuisance to the man so falsely accused and his family, it also tarnishes their reputation. This in turn becomes a great threat that a household may face **(20).** The employer's perspective holds equal importance as well. It has been pointed out, that in light of the increased number of complaints since the passing of this Act, the employers feel discouraged from hiring women all together. More and more employers shall not prefer the unnecessary risk of any such allegations and would in fact hire a male employee. This could result a great step backward in providing equal opportunity to women, ultimately hurting them in a perverse manner **(21).** With the reducing trend of gender exclusiveness at various workplaces, more and more men and women are interacting with each other at workplaces. This trend has led to an indispensible need to create a freer and friendly environment for both genders to freely interact and communicate. Humour within limits, can sometimes be stress reliever. However with the strict provisions of the new law, it appears as though this easy interaction will get curbed. With employees being much more careful with their jokes, it will ultimately create a hostile environment at workplace. Circumstances where casual relations are encouraged between men and women will be curbed due to fear of it being misconceived.

Conclusions:

In most sexual harassment in the workplace cases, the victims are angry, annoyed, and embarrassed by theunwanted sexual attention. The victim may face psychological trauma, anxiety, nervousness, sadness, depression,and the feeling of low self – esteem. Some common effects of sexual harassment are decreased workperformance, increased absenteeism, loss of job and income, having one's personal life offered up for publicscrutiny (the victim becomes the accused), and their dress, lifestyle, and private life will often come under attack,being objectified and humiliated by scrutiny and gossip, and others. A worker who faces sexual harassment oftenchooses to resign as revealing it would tarnish and humiliate their image. As a result they suffer it alone and insilence. Sexual harassment in the workplace should be regarded as a serious matter and should be tackled moreeffectively. For these reasons, the researcher believe enacting a comprehensive and effective legislation on theissue of sexual harassment in the workplace is important because such legislation will have a positive effect instamping out sexual advancement in the workplace and eventually will create a more safe and healthy workingenvironment.

REFERENCES

1. Mackinnon, C.A. (1979): Sexual harassment of working women: A case of sex discrimination. Vol-19, New Haven, Yale University Press.
2. Fitzgerald, L.F., Shullman, S., Bailey, N., Richards, M., Swecker, J., Gold, A., Ormerod, A.J., and Weitzman, L. (1988): The incidence and dimensions of sexual harassment in academia and the workplace. Journal of Vocational Behaviour. 32.152-175.
3. Farley (1978): Sexual Shakedown: The Sexual Harassment of Women on Job. New York:McGraw-Hill, 9-18.
4. Fitzgerald, L.F. (1993): Sexual Harassment: Violence Against Women in the Workplace. American Psychologist, 48,1070-1076.
5. Fitzgerald, L.F., Shullman, S., Bailey, N., Richards, M., Swecker, J., Gold, A., Ormerod, A.J., and Weitzman, L. (1988): The incidence and dimensions of sexual harassment in academia and the workplace. Journal of Vocational Behaviour. 32.152-175.
6. Studd, M.V. and Gattiker, U.E. (1991): The Evolutionary Psychology of Sexual Harassment in Organizations, Ethology and Socio-biology, 12(4), 249-290.

7. Mackinnon, C.A. (1979): Sexual harassment of working women: A case of sex discrimination. Vol-19, New Haven, Yale University Press.
8. Tangri,S.S., Burt, M.R. and Johnson, L.B. (1982): Sexual Harassment at Work: Three Explanatory Models. Journal of Social Issues, 38(4),33-54.
9. Gruber, J.E. (1992): The sexual harassment experiences of women in non-traditional jobs: Results from cross-national research. In proceedings of the First National Conference on sex and power issues in the workplace. Bellevue, WA.
10. Cleveland, J.M. and Kerst, M.E. (1993): Sexual harassment and perception of power: An under-articulated relationship. Journal of Vocational Behaviour.
11. Gutek,B.A. and Morasch, B. (1982): Sex-ratios, sex-role spill over and sexual harassment of women at work. Journal of Social Issues, 38(4), 55-74.
12. Gutek, B.A., Cohen, A.G. and Knorad, A.M. (1990): Predicting social-sexual behaviour at work: A contact-hypothesis. Academy of Management Journal,33, 560-577.
13. Gutek, B.A., Cohen, A.G. and Knorad, A.M. (1990): Predicting social-sexual behaviour at work: A contact-hypothesis. Academy of Management Journal, 33, 560-577.
14. www.secasa@monashhealth.org
15. www.secasa@monashhealth.org
16. www.secasa@monashhealth.org
17. www.secasa@monashhealth.org
18. Kathryn Abrams (1989): Gender Discrimination and the Transformation of Workplace Norms, Vanderbilt L. Rev., Vol.42, 1207-1209.
19. Rule 6 (i) of the Sexual Harassment of Women at Workplace (Prevention, Prohibition and Redressal) Rules, 2013
20. Are sexual harassment laws enough? *available at* http://www.mid-day.com/articles/are-sexual-harassment-laws-enough/15077056.
21. Workplace Act could end up hurting women *available at* http://blogs.economictimes.indiatimes.com/SilkStalkings/entry/workplace-act-could-end-up-hurting-women.

2

Evolution of the Concept of HRM from the Functional to the Strategic Importance of the Organizations and the Role of Management Education in Its Change Process

Dr. Kaushik Kundu & Dr. Dev Narayan Sarkar

ABSTRACT

The concept of Human Resource Management has evolved over a long period of time since the beginning of the 20th century. From the concept of the welfare of the workers Human Resource Management has been established as a tactical instrument of people empowerment in workplace. HRM has emerged as a management concept that helps mangers to plan, recruit, select, train, develop, remunerate and maintain people for an organization. But in the global business scenario HRM is being redefined as a strategic management concept. While getting relieved from a large number of its prototype classical functions HRM is now playing a key role in formulation, implementation, and evaluation of the sets of long term strategies at the functional level, business level, and the corporate level of the organizations. In this changing scenario management education must identify and incorporate the redefined conceptual changes of HRM to train the future HR managers.

Key Words: Personnel Management, Labour Welfare, Human Resource Management, Management Education

Introduction:

Over a period of years multinational corporations are setting up businesses across the globe facilitated by the removal of trade barriers, technology, capital, and people. The past two decades have witnessed the emergence of economies like China, India, Russia, Brazil, and Mexico. India is appearing as an important global hub for businesses. Indian corporate houses like the Tata, Birla, Reliance, Wipro, and Mahindra are growing both in and outside of the country. Human resources are playing the role of key enablers in the growth of the organizations. One of the important conditions of success has become the competent organizational members who can undertake and implement the challenges of managing in the global context. Hence human resource and its management have become a strategic issue to the organizations. The organizations' expectations from the management academics are also changing with this changing scenario. We can try to trace the pattern of changes evolving over the period.

Evolution of the Concept of HRM:

To trace back the historical concept, HRM as a concept is relatively new that has emerged during the 1970s. Even still a large number of managers refer to the discipline by its traditional titles such as labour administration, personnel administration, or personnel management. The welfare concept of employees in business organizations exists since the introduction of the concept of management. Still in the countries like India under imperialistic colonialism where organized industries had started to flourish only at the end of 19th or the beginning of 20th century, concepts like "labour welfare" were more a myth than reality. The concept has started to receive its due importance since the First World War and the Bolshevik Revolution in Russia with the emergence of trade union movement in the country and growing awareness among the workers about their rights. The Royal Commission of Labour in 1931 came up with a number of recommendations along with the recommendation of appointment of a labour welfare officer. Based on these recommendations and the conventions of International Labour Organization, the government introduced "the Factories Act, 1934" giving a number of conditions regarding workers working in factories and made the appointment of welfare officers compulsory ("The Factories Act, 1948"). After the Second World War the trade union movement in the country became more intensified and employees became more aware of their employment conditions and rights. After independence and through the 50s and 60s, the personnel function began to expand crossing the limit of welfare and the other administrative functions like personnel procurement, training, evaluation or appraisal of performance, industrial relations, salary administration, discipline of employees have come under the same concept and the new branch is being called personnel management. Over the decades the concept of personnel management has also undergone modifications and new areas like career planning, manpower planning have been included inside its operational and strategic functions. During 90s the philosophical emphasis has modified to human value orientated management and people empowerment in workplace. This gave rise to the concept of Human Resource Management (HRM). To define formally, HRM is a management concept that helps managers plan, recruit, select, train, develop, remunerate and maintain people for an organization.

The Changing Role of HRM:

1. The human resource of an organization has been highlighted as one of the strategic strength of any organization to be globally competitive. Human Resource Management as a tool is also undergoing modification to handle the competitive and efficient human resource.

Maintaining the human resource is no longer viewed as the sacred duty of the HR manager in the organization. For day to day interactions, employees largely depend upon their immediate superior and he as a line manager becomes accountable for motivation, or other behavioural issues of his subordinates. The core HR department of the organization has a little role to play over there. Even in the other HR issues like discipline, grievance handling, identification of the training needs, etc. the active participation of the line supervisors has become essential.

2. Planning of human resource with all its quantitative projections and measurements have become much easier for the managers with the development of the software like SAP, PeopleSoft, ManSoft, etc. Use of the statistical techniques in the forecast of human resource demand or the forecast of human resource supply has become more or less a routine job with the use of software packages.

Even in the other areas like performance management, training and development the exclusivity and the workload of HR managers are much reduced due to the participation of the line managers or the extensive use of technology.

3. The above developments in the human resource management domain of the business enterprises have initiated the change of conventional HRM towards the strategic HRM or SHRM. In the strategic perspective, HRM goes beyond and focuses on partnership with internal and external constituents groups **(Mello, 2003)**. It refers to the processes of developing policies, programs, and practices to attain the organizational objectives in the long run and consequently more aligned to the organizational vision and mission. Strategic human resource management analyses and translates the enterprise business strategies into specific people based management operations and systems. In the view to analyze strategic HRM the exploration of the core concept of strategic management is important.

Strategic Management: Concept

1. Strategic management may be defined as the art and science of formulating, implementing, and evaluating cross-functional decisions that enable an organization to achieve its objectives **(David, 2005)**. As the definition implies, strategic management focuses on integrating marketing, finance, operations, and computer information systems to achieve organizational objectives. The process of strategic management consists of three stages: strategy formulation, strategy implementation, and strategy evaluation. Strategy formulation includes developing a

Fig.1: A Comprehensive Strategic- Management Model

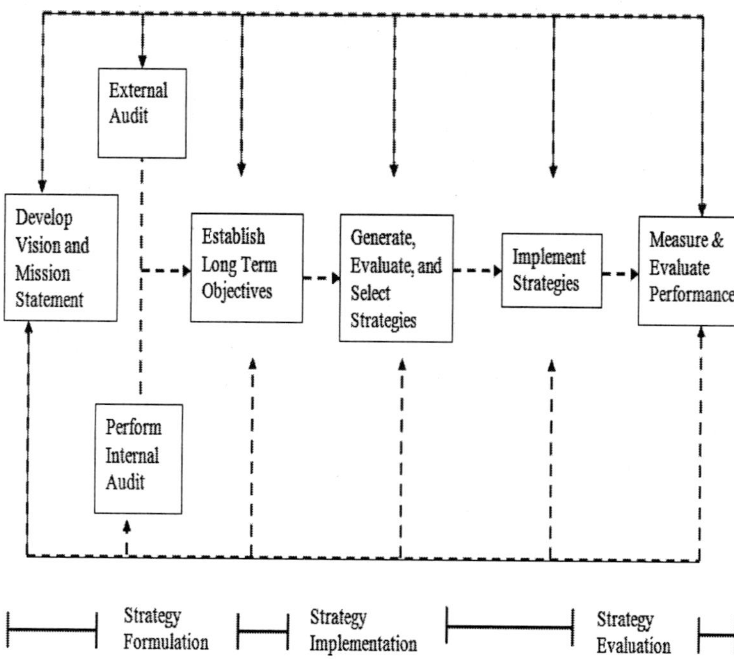

Source: Ferd David, "How Companies Define Their Mission," Long Range Planning 22, no.3 (June, 1988): 40

vision and mission, conducting the SWOT analysis and analyzing results, establishing long term objectives, generating strategies, etc. Strategy formulation includes deciding on new ventures, expansion of business, diversification of market, allocation of resources etc. Evaluation includes taking periodic feedback, deciding on appropriate control system, etc. The process of strategic management in any enterprise can be studied with the help of the model provided by **David (1988)**.

2. The identification of an organization's vision, mission, objectives, and strategies is the starting point of the strategic management of any business enterprise. Every organization has its own sets of vision, mission, or objectives though they may not always be formally documented.

The process of strategic management is continuous and dynamic and the selection, implementation, and evaluation of strategies use to come sequentially after setting the long term objectives of the firm. The whole process is monitored through internal and external audit whose feedback becomes essential in going into the next stage of strategic management.

As expressed in the model *developing a mission statement* is the beginning step of the strategic management. The process must involve the employees of the organization. Through involvement, people become committed to an organization. The process of developing a mission statement should create an "emotional bond" and "sense of mission" between the organization and its employees (Campbell & Yeung, 1991). An emotional bond emerges when an employee individually can identify himself with the underlying values and behavior of the organization. Consequently the realization results into intellectual agreement and commitment to strategy and manifests as a sense of mission.

The purpose of the *external audit* is to formulate a finite list of opportunities that could benefit a firm and threats that would have to be eliminated or avoided, depending on the situation. It is not aimed at developing an exhaustive list of every possible factor that would have positive or negative influence on the business. It is rather aimed at identifying the key variables that offers measurable responses.

All the organizations have strong and weak functional areas of business. No organization is uniformly strong or weak in all the areas. Internal strengths and weaknesses along with external opportunities and threats backed by the mission statement provide the functional basis of setting objectives and formulating strategies for an organization. *Internal audit* as shown in the model identifies the strong and weak areas for the organization.

Long term objectives are the outcomes of the strategies. Strategies represent the actions to be taken to accomplish the long term objectives. The predecided time frame for objectives and strategies must be consistent and synchronized. In the absence of the long term objectives the organization would drift aimlessly and the outcomes will be uncertain.

As shown in the model the next stage is the *generation, evaluation, and selection of strategies*. Strategy analysis demands to determine alternative courses of actions that would best enable an organization to achieve its long term objectives aligned with its mission. The set of formulated strategies, objectives and mission combined with the internal and external audit information, provide the basis for generating and evaluating alternative feasible sets of strategies. The essence of strategy formulation is an assessment of whether a firm is in the right path and how effective its future actions can be.

Strategy implementation is the next stage in the model. Successful strategy formulation can not guarantee successful implementation. Implementing strategies require such actions like hiring new employees, development of new products, financial budgets, training employees, remodeling MIS system of the organization etc. Successful strategy implementation depends on cooperation and coordination among all functional and departmental divisions of an organization.

The best-formulated and best implemented strategies become obsolete as a firm's external and internal environments change. It is therefore essential that the strategies are reviewed, evaluated, and controlled. *Strategy evaluation* includes the following activities: (1) examination of the underlying bases of a firm's strategy (2) comparison of the expected result with the actual result (3) corrective actions. Effective strategy evaluation allows an organization to capitalize on internal strength, to exploit external opportunities, to recognize and eliminate threats, and to cover internal weaknesses.

3. Strategic management allows an organization to make effective long term decisions, to make effective excisions of these decisions, to take corrective actions to ensure results.

The generalized model though applicable for all the management functions but the key adaptation of the model is best suited for strategic HRM.

Human Resource Role in Strategic Management or Strategic Human resource management:

1. Strategic Human Resource Management may also be interpreted following the same model of David. The model starts with the internal and external audits. In Human Resource context HR Audit is done internally, and a SWOT analysis of people covers the internal and external factors for the organization.

In the second step of strategy formulation HRM concentrates at the three levels:

Corporate Level: Different strategies related to the future development of the firm like mergers, horizontal and vertical integration, conglomerate diversification, may be formulated at this stage. Even backward strategies like liquidation, stoppage of operations are also included at the corporate level.

Business Level: A business unit of a firm may be considered as a subsystem having a specific market, a set of distinct customers, a set of competitors, and a specific set of objectives that may be differentiated from the similar sets of the other sub systems operating under the same firm. They are known as Strategic Business Units (SBU). Human Resource Management of these subsystems can participate in the various strategic decisions of the business units.

Functional Level: Each of the Business units of any firm consists of several functional departments like marketing, operation and production, finance etc. Human resource management at the functional level formulates the functional strategies in collaboration and consultation with the other functional departments.

2. At the third stage the formulated strategies need to be implemented at the different levels. Implementation of strategies involve various actions like procurement of human resource, designing training and development program, formulating employee benefits, transfer, promotion, redeployment, etc. HRM equips the enterprise with a very competent workforce and build up inventories of relevant knowledge, appropriate skills, and proper attitude. These inventories collectively termed as the human resource of an organization are responsible for the implementation of the strategies at various levels. Moreover the human resource management of the units can implement strategies at the following areas like productivity, goal integration, total quality management (TQM), total productivity maintenance (TPM), industrial safety, quality circle etc.

3. The third stage is strategic human resource management evaluation. Here the human resource management is assuming a very crucial role. The strategic areas like performance management, training need

identification, training evaluation, various audits for organization HR plays a very critical role. Being not involved with any line activity directly, HRM can assume the role of impartial observer to evaluate the strategies at various levels in the organization.

Fig: 2 Strategic HR Model

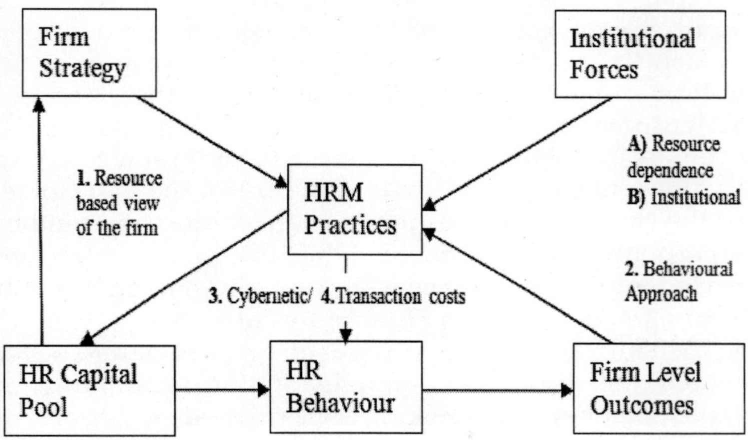

Source: Charles R. Greer, *Strategic Human Resource Management*, 2006

4. The above model represents the comprehensive framework of strategic HRM. The model presents six variables, four of which, provide explanations for practices resulting from strategy orientation of the organization. First, the resource based perspective, explains practices that provide competitive advantages, such as the allocation of firm's resources, organizational culture, core competencies. The second variable, a behavioural approach explains practices that are designed to control and influence attitude and behavior. The third variable draws on the cybernetic systems. This explains the adoption of practices resulting from feedback on contributions to strategy. Transaction cost variable the fourth one explains the use of control systems such as appraisal system etc.

The other two variables in the model A) resource dependence and B) institutional forces are not driven by strategy consideration but act as the external influencing variable.

Management Education and SHRM:

From the noble responsibility of the welfare of the employees the concept of HRM has covered along way to reach the strategic significance in the management of modern organizations. For a long time the B school curriculum has emphasized too much on the tools, techniques, enactments, methods, and programs to equip the future managers to direct and control the workforce. But the strategic part has never been emphasized neither the curriculum has been molded to fit this current enterprise demand into HR mainstream. Of course in some curriculum paper named "Strategic Human Resource Management" has been introduced but the particular course design never covered the issues like implementation, evaluation in detailed manner. The changing scenario demands extensive remodeling to prepare the future HR managers for the changing scenario.

REFERENCES

1. Agarwal, R. D. (1977), *Dynamics of Personnel Management in India,* Tata McGraw-Hill Publishing Co. New Delhi.
2. Aswathappa, K. (2007), *Human Resource Management Text and Cases,* Tata McGraw-Hill Publishing Co. New Delhi.
3. Basu, K. S. (1979), *New Dimensions in Personnel Management,* Macmillan & Co. New Delhi.
4. David, F. R. (1988), "How Companies Define Their Mission," *Long Range Planning,* Vol. 22. No. 3.
5. David, F. R. (2005), *Strategic Management, concepts and cases,* Prentice-Hall of India, New Delhi.
6. Flippo, E. B. (1984), *Personnel Management,* 4th ed. McGraw-Hill, New York.
7. Greer, C. R. (2006), *Strategic Human Resource Management,* Pearson, Singapore.

8. Mello, J. A. (2003), *Strategic Human Resource Management*, Thomson.
9. Ramaswamy, E. A. (1986), "From IR to HRD", *Business India*, April 21-May 4.
10. Thomson, A. A. and Strickland, A. J. (2003), *Strategic Management*, Tata McGraw-Hill Publishing Co. New Delhi.

3

Retail Sales Effectiveness of Retail Outlet (Petrol Pump) of Oil Marketing Company as one of the keys to Performance Management

Dr. Pradip Paul

ABSTRACT

A network of Channel partners, Dealers, Distributors and franchisees are considered to be one of the most effective finished product distribution system for reaching the finished products from manufacturing points to end consumers. Distribution channel is a chain of businesses or intermediaries through which a good or service passes until it reaches the final buyer or the end consumer.Distribution channels can include wholesalers, retailers, distributors etc. It may have one tier system like ware house to retailer directly or may have different tiers in between.The performance of the Retailers, Channel partners or dealers who directly interacts with end consumers of the finished products has been studied in this research paper. An approach towards measure of Retail Sales Effectiveness as functions of Market Participation (P) and Market Share (S)has been considered in this paper. A Retail networkfor catering petroleum gasoline products especially Motor Spirit and High-Speed Diesel popularly known as Petrol and Diesel in India, has been considered for the study. The individual business entity of Retail network is known as Petrol Pumps or Retail Outlets in most of the parts of the country. The owner of the petrol pump is generally called as Dealer. In this study retail sales effectiveness of petrol pump's dealer or effectiveness of Retail Outlets have been emphasized as measure to Dealer performance management.Moreover, the effectiveness of OMCs is also studied where effectiveness of Dealer or Retail Outlet is integral part of it.

Keywords: Retail Sales,Oil Marketing Company, Petrol and Diesel, Performance Management

Introduction:

In most of the country's petroleum products are considered as energy fuels and are mostly marketed as LPG, Naptha, MS, ATF, SKO, HSD, LDO, Lubricants&

Fig. 1.1: Consumption of Petroleum products in India from Fin 1998-99 to 2018-19

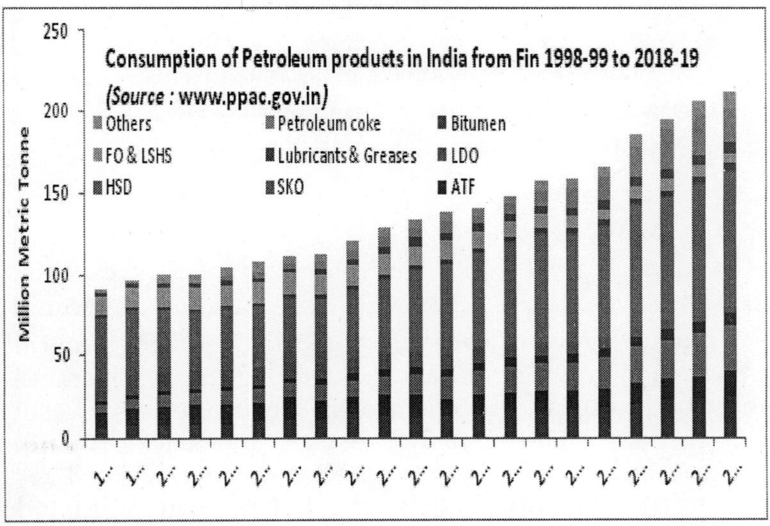

Greases, FO & LSHS, Bitumen and Petroleum Coke. The trend of consumption of above products in last twenty years as collected from Petroleum Planning and Analysis Cell (PPAC)[1] under Minsitry of Petroelum and Natural Gas (MOPNG) has been shown in Fig 1.1.

It is evident that consumption of Petrol and Diesels is considerably high and contributes as important energy fuel in India. Fig 1.2,shows an graphical representation of year wise percentage consumption of Petrol and Diesel of total consumption of petroleum products in India based on the data presented in Fig 1.1. It has been observed that petrol and diesel plays an important role as energy fuels in Indian Economy with more than 50% of total petroleum products in last ten years.

Fig. 1.2: Trend of Percentage Consumption of Petrol and Diesel of Total consumption of Petroleum Products in India

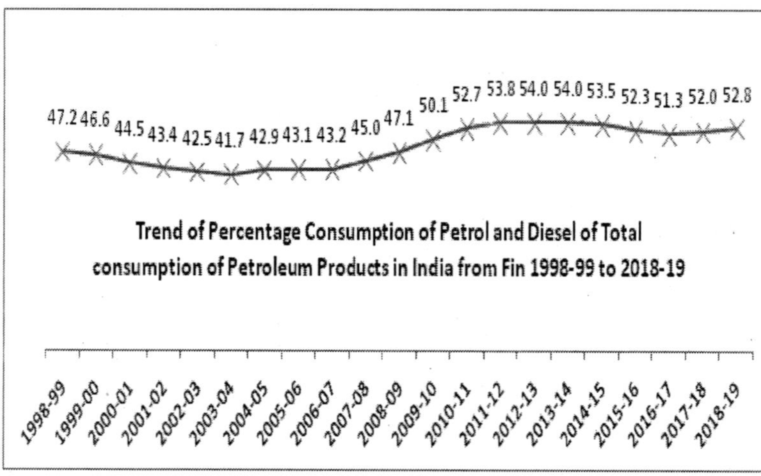

Petrol i.e. Motor Spirit is primarily used by general public's in their two stroke and Four stroke engines operated motor bikes and marketed through Retail Outlets. Diesel ie High Speed Diesel (HSD) is used by Trucks, Buses, Tractors, DG sets, Diesel operated machineries used for Industries, Agricultural belts etc. It has been estimated that more than 90% and 80% of MS and HSD respectively are marketed through Retail Outlet or so-called Petrol Pumps in India.

Petrol and Diesel are generally produced from Refineries which process crude oils. The total upstream and downstream process requires huge investments, skilled human resources, sophisticated technology know how, compliance of different government and statutory regulations on Health, safety and environments (HSE). India being a country with low reserve of crude oil, it depends on import of crudes. Govt. of India with majority stakes operates state run oil companies, Indian Oil Corporation Ltd (IOCL), Bharat Petroleum Corporation Ltd (BPCL) and Hindustan Petroleum Corporation Ltd (HPCL) as downstream Oil Marketing Companies. After deregularization of Retail Outlets and withdraw of administrative pricing mechanism (APM), other private entrepreneurs like Reliance India Ltd, Essar, Shell etc have invested in setting up refineries and started their Retail network. The corporate operating in downstream business of petroleum products, mainly marketing of Petrol, Diesel, Lubricants and Greases through Retail Outlets are known as Oil Marketing Company (OMC). Though the profitability of the OMCs is dependent on crude prices in international markets but sale of Petrol and Diesel through Retail Outlets plays an important role both in profitability, operational flexibility and sustainability of refineries as most of the OMCs operates on huge capital investment. After withdraw of APM, OMCs were empowered to expand their network by setting up more Retail Outlets based on the potential and socio-economic feasibility. The above has resulted almost exponential growth of numbers of Retail Outlets in India from 45104 in 2012 to 64625 in 2019 as per information available in Petroleum Planning and Analysis Cell (PPAC). As there is a high volatility of crude oil prices price in international market, hence profitabilityof Retail Outlet is generally not considered for Retail effectiveness. But considering expansion of Retail network and increase in demand of Petrol and Diesel it is essential to decide a simple tool to study effectiveness of a Retail Outlet in the respective market and effectiveness of Retail network of a particular OMC.

Market Segmentation

A, Caroline Tynan and Jennifar Drayton, had rightly stated in one of them publication long back that market segmentation is a crucial marketing strategy and its aim is to identify and delineate market segments or "sets of buyers" which would then become the targets for the company's marketing plans [2]. The Retail Outlets are situated both in rural and urban areas with access from public roads. The size and layout of Retail Outlet is governed by different statutory requirements stipulated by Government bodies and functional requirement by OMCs. The primary business objective of Retail Outlet is to cater MS, HSD, Lubricants and Greases to the customers. Based on the socio-geographical condition of the customer catchment, the OMCs maintains almost uniform market classification. The classifications of markets are presented in Fig 2.1.

Fig 2.1: Classification of markets

Class A	Class B	Class C	Class D	Class E
• Metropolitan cities and other cities / towns having population >20 lakhs as per 2011 census.	• Cities having a population > 4 lakhs to 20 lakhs as per 2011 census.	• All other Towns / Cities (Areas covered under Municipal limits of a town) not covered under "A" & "B" class markets and locations not on Highways (NH/SH)	• Natioanl and State Highways	• Rural areas (Areas not covered under Municipal limits of a town) other than A, B, C & D Class of markets.

Classification of markets is necessary to understand the requirement of customers and it is directional to OMCs for deciding layout and facility mapping. Further the markets are sub grouped to study the effectiveness in micro level. In micro level, the most popular concept which all OMCs are following is Trading Area Mapping.

Trading Area Mapping is primarily a group of ROs with more or less similar business characteristics, customers mix and having uniform potential.For example, consider a schematic diagram as shown in Fig 2.2, where a Stretch of National Highway has been shown. The ROs are numbered as M_iR_j where Mi represents the ithOMC and Rj represents jth Retail Outlet. The national highway is marked as NH-X. Different cities or landmark are identified as A, B, C, D, E and F. Major junction or intersection with other Roads towards different cities are marked as J1 and J2.

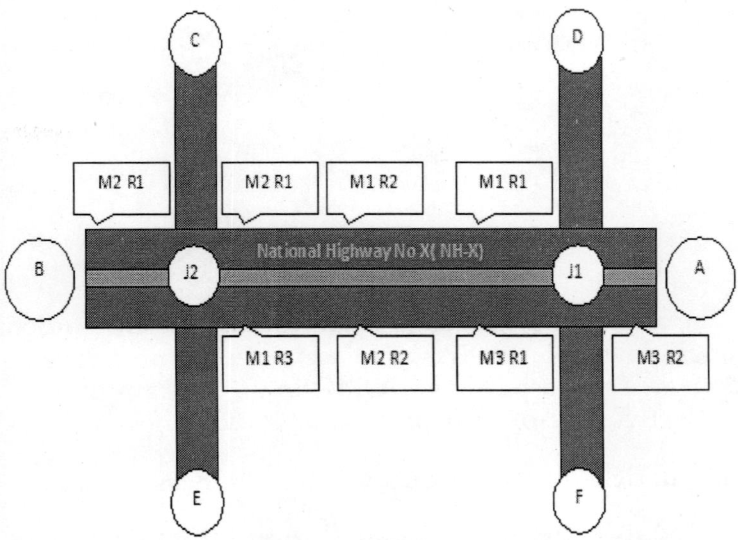

Fig2.2 : Scematic diagram of NH-X with location of ROs, Junctions and Major cities/markets

NH-X as shown is a divided carriageway. Hence the traffic characteristics are different on left- and right-hand side of NH-X. Moreover, there are traffic diversion towards C, E and D,F from junction J2 and J1 respectively.

Therefore, between J1 and J2, the ROs can be mapped in two Trading Areas (TA) as shown in Fig 2.3. M2R1 and M3R2 are not considered in the above TAs as business characteristics are changed due to road intersection at junctions J1 and J2.

Fig 2.3:Trading Area Mapping

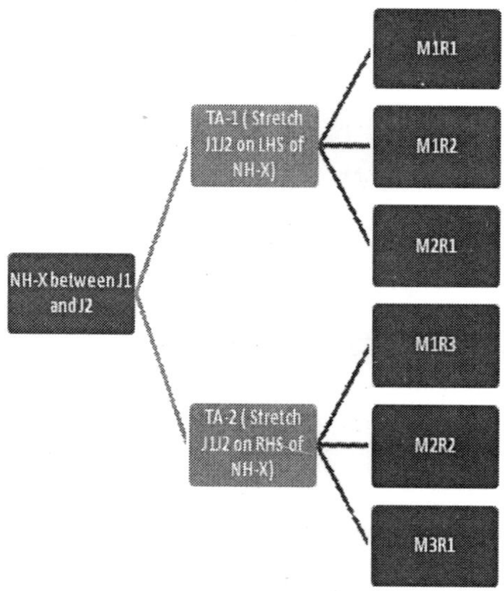

The effectiveness of Retail Outlet and OMCs are studied in micro levels in the TAs. The weighted summations of effectiveness of a particular OMC in all TAs are used to get effectiveness of that particular OMC.

Mathematical Formulations of Effectiveness

All OMCs are being operated under the umbrella of MOPNG and an authentic, validated system exists in sharing district and RO wise sales data among OMCs.

Each OMC maintains TA distribution of ROs as described above. Mathematical formulation of RO and OMC effectiveness is very simple and powerful tool to drill down further to improve the retaii network.

The mathematical formulation is basically atwo-pillaramalgamation leading to a conclusive, comparable number known as Effectiveness as shown in Fig.3.1

Fig: 3.1 Two pillar concept of effectiveness

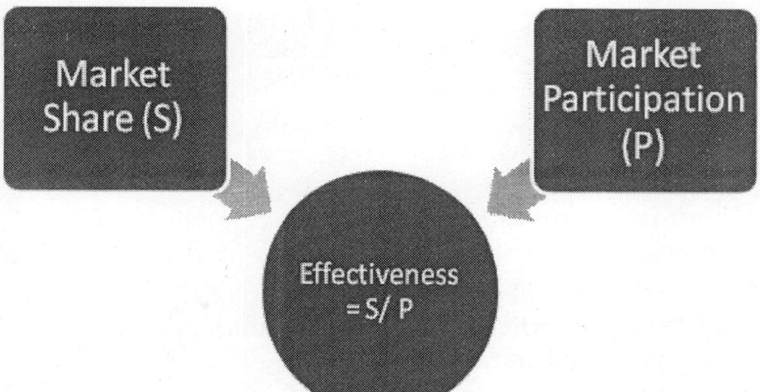

Table 3.1 : TA wise sample sales data

TA Number	TA name	Class of market	District	OMC Name	RO name	Sales (KLPM)
TA1	Stretch J1J2 on LHS of NH-X	D	X	M1	M1R1	500
		D	X	M1	M1R2	850
		D	X	M2	M2R1	1000
TA2	Stretch J1J2 on RHS of NH-X	D	X	M1	M1R3	400
		D	X	M2	M2R2	600
		D	X	M3	M3R1	550

The Market Share (S) refers to a RO's or OMC's portion of sales within the TA. Market participation (P)basically refers to the presence of one OMC in comparison to the total presence of OMC. The S and P can be explained with hypothetical assumptions of sales figure of ROsin TAs as shown in Fig. 2.3 and as tabulated in Table 3.1.

The S of each RO is calculated as percentage sales of the particular RO of the total sales of the trading area. Mathematically it can be expressed as

$$S^{TAk\,(k=1,2,3.....)}_{Mi\,(i=1,2,3...)Rj(j=1,2,3....)} = \frac{\sum Sales\ of\ Mi\,(i=1,2,3...)Rj(j=1,2,3....)}{\sum_{i=1,n}^{j=1,n} Sales\ of\ MiRj} \quad \text{Eq 3.1}$$

Summation of RO market share of same OMC will give market share of particular OMC in the TA.

Similarly, market participation of each RO is calculated as percentage of participation of the RO under consideration in the TA. Mathematically it can be expressed as

$$P^{TAk\,(k=1,2,3.....)}_{Mi\,(i=1,2,3...)Rj(j=1,2,3....)} = \frac{1}{\sum_{i=1,n}^{j=1,n} Count\ of\ MiRj} \quad \text{Eq 3.2}$$

The market participation of an OMC is calculated as multiplication of count of particular OMC with the market participation of each RO in the TA.

The market share (S) and market participation (P) as calculated from the above equation for the sample data presented in Table 3.1 has been shown in Fig 3.2 to Fig 3.5.

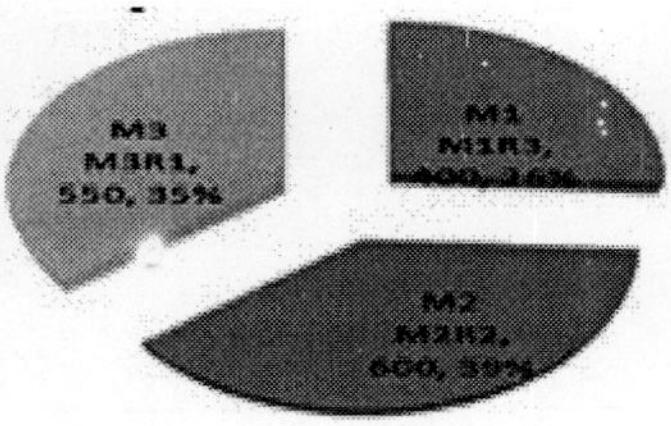

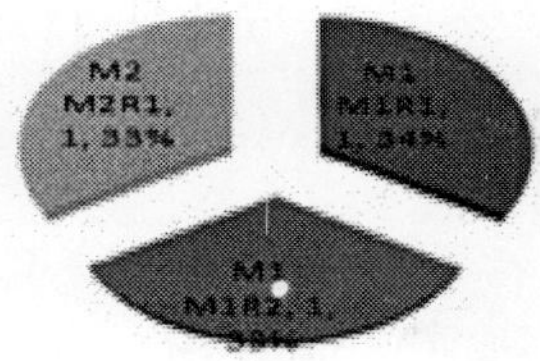

Fig 3.3 : Market Share (S) of TA2 Fig 3.4 : Market Participation (P) of TA1

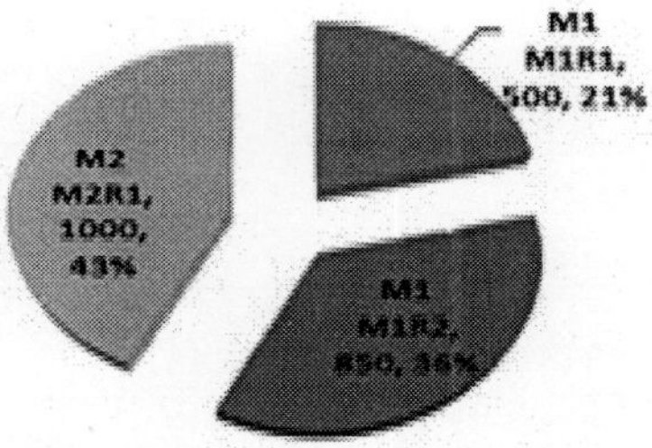

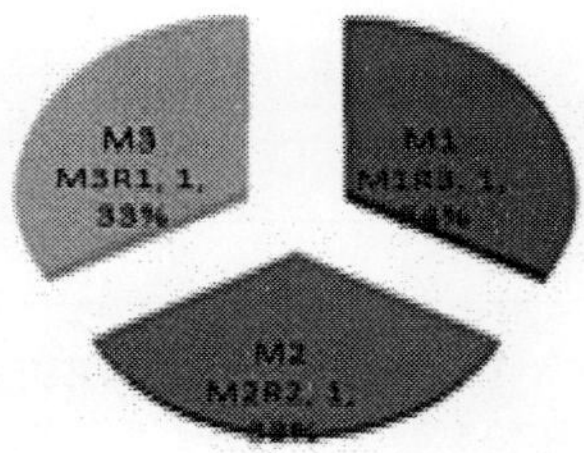

Fig 3.2 : Market Share (S) of TA1 Fig 3.5: Market Participation (P) of TA2

Based on the above, the Effectiveness of a particular RO and OMC can be calculated by market share (S) upon Market participation (P). The sample calculation of effectiveness based on the data assumed in Table 3.1 is presented in Table 3.2 to Table 3.5.

Table 3.2 : Effectiveness of Retail Outlet

TA Number	TA name	Class of market	District	OMC Name	RO name	S	P	Effectiveness (S/P)
TA1	Stretch J1J2 on LHS of NH-X	D	X	M1	M1R1	21	34	0.62
		D	X	M1	M1R2	36	33	1.09
		D	X	M2	M2R1	43	33	1.30
TA2	Stretch J1J2 on RHS of NH-X	D	X	M1	M1R3	26	34	0.76
		D	X	M2	M2R2	39	33	1.18
		D	X	M3	M3R1	35	33	1.06

Table 3.3 : TA wise Effectiveness of OMC

TA Number	TA name	Class of market	District	OMC Name	∑S	∑P	Effectiveness (S/P)
TA1	Stretch J1J2 on LHS of NH-X	D	X	M1	57	67	0.85
		D	X	M2	43	33	1.30
TA2	Stretch J1J2 on RHS of NH-X	D	X	M1	26	34	0.76
		D	X	M2	39	33	1.18
		D	X	M3	35	33	1.06

Table 3.4 : Effectiveness of OMC in the market comprising of TA1 and TA2

TA Number	TA name	Class of market	District	OMC Name	∑S= ∑Sales Mi/ ∑Sales TA %	∑P=Count Mi x (1/Total Count M)%	Effectiveness (S/P)
TA1 & TA2	Stretch J1J2 on LHS of NH-X & Stretch J1J2 on RHS of NH-X	D	X	M1	45	50	0.90
				M2	41	33	1.23
				M3	14	17	0.85

Result and Discussion

The above result based on the sample example given in Table 3.1, a market analyst may conclude effectiveness of a Retail Outlet and OMC. The effectiveness should preferably be more than 1.0, implies it should have market share more than market participation. OMC may tabulate market effectiveness of TAs, Districts, marketwise for each RO and combined for the OMC. Wherever market effectiveness of OMC is coming less than 1.0, OMC should focus in that particular market or market segment. Further in that particular market segment, OMC may drill down to RO wise effectiveness. The ROs with effectiveness less than 1.0 are identified. OMC along with dealer/channel partners of the ROs, formulate strategy to improve effectiveness. In this process sometimes, dealer/ channel partners with growing trends are also found not effective up to the mark if their growth is less than the combined growth in the market segment. The above simple procedure is very much helpful in identifying the market segment where an Oil Marketing Company should focus to improve retail effectiveness. Moreover, it helps the management to prepare a comparative performance model of dealer/ channel partners for taking them onboard during panel discussion.

REFERENCES

1. www.ppac.gov.in (Petroleum Planning & Analysis Cell).
2. Tynan, A. C. & Jenifer, D. (1987). Market Segmentation. *Journal of Marketing Management*, 2(3). 301-335.
3. McNair, C.J. and Mosconi, W. (1987), 'Measuring performance in an advanced manufacturing environment', *Management Accounting*, 69 (1), pp. 28-31.
4. McAdam, R., Hazlett, S. & Casey, C. (2005), 'Performance management in the UK public sector: Addressing multi stakeholder complexity', *International Journal of Public Sector Management*, 18(3), pp. 256–273.
5. Reyna, M., & Sims, R.R. (1995), 'A framework for individual management development in the public sector', *Public Personnel Management*, 24(1), 53-65.
6. Reinke, S.J. (2003), 'Does the form really matter? Leadership, trust, and acceptance of the performance appraisal process', *Review of Public Personnel Administration*, 23(1), 23-37.
7. Snell S. and George Bohlander G.W. (2007), Human Resource management, 14th edition, Cengage learning, New York.
8. Rowley, J. (2002), 'Using case studies in research', *Management Research News*, 25(1), pp.16-27.
9. SOCAR, Economics & Statistics: Oil Production, (2016), Baku, Azerbaijan.

4

Convergence in Income through the Passage of Human Capital in the Indian States: 1960-2005

Dr. Santanu Ray Chaudhuri

ABSTRACT

This paper tries to concentrate on the issue of convergence under neoclassical paradigm across Indian states through the passage of human capital variables during the period between 1960 and 2005. The paper tries to address the issue in a broad landscape to scrutinize the issue including dynamic model through the passage of human capital variables in different frameworks with controlled time and state-specific effects in different growth episodes. The outcomes emphasize the significance of policy mechanism to achieve balanced growth and regional convergence in Indian states.

Keywords: Human Capital; Inequality; Convergence; Indian States; Growth

Introduction:

The neoclassical argument of economic growth primarily focuses on steady-state growth rate which is independent of initial conditions, and, per capita output growth depends only on the exogenous growth of technology and growth of labour force. If technology is a public good, then all the economies will rest on the same steady-state with same per capita growth of output in long run. The basic reason behind the argument is the well-known neo-classical assumption of diminishing returns of the factors of production. This implies that the poor economies will grow faster and their per capita income growth would become equal to those of rich ones. Thus when all the economies would converge towards the same steady-state in terms of per capita growth rate of income, then this is called absolute â-convergence. Hence, the basic proposition of the neo-classical framework is that economies converge in the long run irrespective to their initial conditions. In absolute â-convergence, the growth of real per capita income is inversely related to the initial real per capita income[1]. But if income per capita is assumed to depend on multiple of structural factors such as human capital, institutions and international trade or efficiency level, then one cannot expect the economies will tend to reach in the same steady state. This means convergence may take place not essentially at the same level in the long-run. This â-convergence is called conditional â-convergence. The conditional convergence hypothesis is backed by huge empirical evidences where it is observed that initial income is negatively related to growth after controlling other explanatory variables. The studies by Barro and Sala-i-Martin (1992), Mankiw *et al.* (1992) and many others have given empirical evidences of conditional â-convergence, although Bernard and Durlauf (1995) have rejected the hypothesis of conditional convergence. Another important feature of neo-classical framework is that agents are assumed to be homogeneous. But if the heterogeneity in agents would be assumed in terms of varied endowments, varied saving ratios out of wage income and capital income, then the dynamical system of the neoclassical model would result in multiple steady-state equilibria despite the assumption of diminishing returns. Galor (1996) with one sector model of overlapping generations and Durlauf and

Johnson (1995) with cross-section data have shown multiple steady-state equilibria. However, the heterogeneous agent assumption in the perspectives of growth model would be more logical, particularly when it has been that human capital potentially plays an effective role on distribution. As the present study primarily examines the issue of convergence among Indian states and takes human capital augmenting variables in the growth regression to scrutinize the perception of multiple steady-state equilibria. Human capital is supposed to be a significant and unique constituent of societal advance, which has both external and spill-over effects. The education variables, in particular, are employed as proxies of it and used as both stock and flow variables as per the needs of the diverse socio-economic researches. The major reason of using of education variables as proxies is that they have one distinctive characteristic to be included as quantifiable components. In their study with overlapping generations model Galor and Zeira (1993) argued that economies with initial unequal distribution of wealth could accumulate lesser human capital and thus subject to lower growth rate than those having more equal distribution of wealth in the hands of vast middle class. Garcia-Penalosa (1995) has studied that increase in inequality lowers the growth rate where cost of education is lower than average holding of wealth. Thus the economies having similar structural determinants as well as initial per capita output and human capital, but unequal in initial distribution would be converged to different steady-state equilibria. Alesina and Rodrik (1994), Persson and Tabellini (1994) and many others have supported this view and the intention of the present study is to test the phenomena in Indian states during the time period between 1960 and 2005. To investigate the link through the passage of different channels, Becker (1962, 1964) and Schultz (1961) have advocated the significance of human capital in the perspective of economic advance. The augmentation of labour by education has been observed in the work of Denison (1967). Uzawa (1965) and Rosen (1976) also described importance of human capital in driving economic growth. According to Nelson and Phelps (1966), the capability of a state to adopt and employ new foreign technology is a function of domestic stock of human capital. The trendiest scheme to proxy the human capital variables are the uses of the stock variables such as literacy rate and school enrolment ratios. Ljungberg (2002) has used enrolment ratio and expenditure on education to scrutinize the pattern of association between education and growth in Sweden during 1867 and 1995. Nunes (2003) has examined the behaviour of public expenditure on education in Portugal between 1852 and 1995. Human capital variables are put in diverse ways with explicit empirical specifications in the works of economists worldwide. Romer (1990) has regressed the growth of GDP on the level of human capital, while Lucas (1988) on the growth of human capital. The issue of human capital to explain long-run growth has also been adequately addressed in the works of Azariadis and Drazen (1990), Barro (1991), Mankiw, Romer, and Weil (1992), Caball´e and Santos (1993), Benhabib and Spiegel (1994), and Fernandez and Rogerson (1995). The present study has also taken per capita public expenditure on education following the 'cost based approach' of human capital formation. The major reason is that public education system in Indian states still covers a major and large portion of entire Indian educational framework and, as such, it is imperative to incorporate the issue government contribution in human capital formation. The comparable dataset of per capita public expenditure on education for the Indian states are by far available for the long run. In the setup of the paper, section 2 examines theoretical background, and Section 3 takes up issues on convergence in India. Section 4 describes graphical representation of convergence perspective given the initial conditions of major eighteen states and section 5 deals with framework and regression analysis. Section 6 sums up the findings and conclusions.

Theoretical Background for Setting up Empirical Analysis:

The production scheme in per capita effective labour in neo-classical framework by Ramsey (1928), Solow (1956), Cass (1965) and Koopmans (1965) is

$\tilde{y}$ = f (k) where $\tilde{y}$ =y/L $^{\lambda t}$ and k= K/L $^{\lambda t}$, λ = exogenously given labour-augmenting technological progress. Hence in the closed economy, k**2** = f (k) - c – (δ + n + λ) k, where ä = depreciation rate and n = growth rate of labour and c = C/ L $^{\lambda t}$.

In the infinite horizon household framework which maximizes U $=\int_0^{\alpha} u(c)e^{nt}e^{-\rho t}dt$, and constant elasticity of marginal utility (say, θ), then in the steady state the per capita variables are grow at the rate λ, and k will satisfy f**2** (k*) = δ + θ λ+ ρ. Now, if the economy starts with k below k*, then k will be monotonically approaches to k*, as per Blanchard and Fischer (1989). According to Barro and Sala-i-Martin (1991), the growth rate of capital per worker tends to decline monotonically towards the steady-state value λ.

Mankiw, Romer and Weil (1992) with Cobb-Douglas form have shown that k2 (t) = s_k y (t) - (n+ g+ δ) k (t) and h2 (t) = s_h y (t) - (n+ g+ δ) h (t) where the production function is of the form

Y (t) = A (t) H (t) $^{\beta}$ K (t) $\varepsilon=\sigma=^{\psi}$ L (t) $^{1-\psi-\beta}$ and L and A grow exogenously at rate n and g. Here H is the stock of human capital and y $=\frac{Y}{AL}$, k $=\frac{K}{AL}$ and h = $\frac{H}{AL}$ and s is saving ratio.

Then the economy converges at the steady-state with

k* = $[\frac{sk^{1-\beta}sh^{\beta}}{n+g+\delta}]^{1/(1-\psi-\beta)}$ and h* = $[\frac{sh^{1-\psi}sk^{\psi}}{n+g+\delta}]^{1/(1-\psi-\beta)}$

Substituting the equations in the production function and taking log obtains steady-state income per capita which is,

$$\ln \left[\frac{Y(t)}{L(t)}\right] = \ln A(0) + g\,t - \left(\frac{\psi+\beta}{(1-\psi-\beta)}\right) \ln (n + g + \delta) + \left(\frac{\psi}{(1-\psi-\beta)}\right) \ln (s_k) + \left(\frac{\beta}{(1-\psi-\beta)}\right) \ln (s_h)$$

This equation explains how income per capita depends on population growth and accumulation of physical and human capital to reach steady state.

Issues of Convergence in India

A large volume of works on convergence in India have come out with conflicting outcomes. One important reason is the variation in the dataset used by the researchers and a huge variation is also observed in taking control variables, time duration as well as in the used regression models. The studies of Cashin and Sahay (1996) and Rao et al. (1999) have shown the indirect perspectives of intergovernmental transfers relating to convergence issue in Indian states. Cashin and Sahay (1996) have shown convergence, but Rao et al. (1999) have shown divergence for same time period, although their dataset are different. Rao et al. (1999) have taken only the fourteen major states, but Cashin and Sahay (1996) have included north-eastern states of India as well as Delhi and Jammu and Kashmir. Dholakia (1994) have argued in favour of convergence of long-term State Domestic Product (SDP) among twenty Indian states during 1960-90 where during 1980, according to him, poorer states have started growing and richer states have started stagnating. The studies by Rao, Shand and Kalirajan (1999) have shown per capita state domestic products are diverging rather than the tendency to converge. The study of Marjit and Mitra (1996) did not find any evidence of convergence on the basis of PCNSDP in twenty four states during the period1961-62 to 1989-90. Ghosh et al. (1998) and Kurian (2000) also argued for regional divergence across states over time. Basu (2002) with the Quality of Governance Index (QGOI) has shown that government quality would be responsible in promoting growth rates between the Indian states.

Initial Conditions and Growth perspectives of Eighteen Major States in India

To test the tendency whether the growth rates of the states have been converging or not, given the initial conditions, the study takes the comparable dataset of PCNSDP and the average growth rates of the eighteen major states over the periods 1060-61 and 2004-05. The horizontal axis of the figure represents the ratio between the base period (1960-61) PCNSDP (x_i) for each state and the average (x-bar) expressed in logarithmic terms. The vertical axis measures the deviations from the average growth rate of PCNSDP (g_i –g-bar). The number corresponding to each state is given below the Figure.

Figure 1: Initial Condition and Trend Line for Seventeen States in India during the Period between 1970-71 and 2004-05:

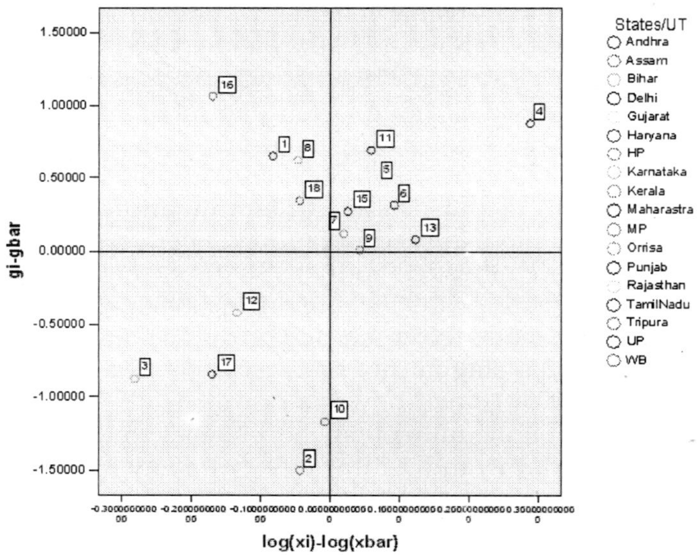

[States in the figure: Andhra (1), Assam (2), Bihar (3), Delhi (4), Gujarat (5), Haryana (6), HP (7), Karnataka (8), Kerala (9), Maharashtra (10), MP (11), Orissa (12), Punjab (13), Rajasthan (14), Tamil Nadu (15), Tripura (16), UP (17), WB(18)]

The figure confers some appealing patterns. First, it is seen that although Andhra, Karnataka, Tripura, HP and West Bengal have started from lower base period income, but have grown moderately faster, while the Maharashtra started with higher base, but did exactly opposite. Assam, Bihar, Orissa and UP started from lower base and grew slower. Second, there is no unambiguous negative relation between the variables, rather shows a rough upward drift, which prima facie substantiates the fact that states in India have not been converging in respect of PCNSDP, rather strong states like Delhi, Gujarat, MP, Punjab, Haryana, Tamil Nadu, Kerala have grown at a faster pace, starting from higher base.

Framework and Econometric Analysis:

The present study has taken two broad set of regressions where log of income ratio as dependent variable and the log of per capita net state domestic product (ln Pcnsdp) of the previous periods are taken as regressors, those calculated from the dataset published by Central Statistical Organization (CSO) at constant price level of 1993-94.

Table 2: Log of Income ratio as Dependent Variable

Sample Period	*Beta-Coefficient of* $ln(y_0)$	*Absolute Convergence/ Divergence*
1960-1965	-0.119	Absolute Convergence
1965-1972	0.362	Absolute Divergence
1972-1977	0.066	Absolute Divergence
1977-1983	0.237	Absolute Divergence
1983-1987	-0.141	Absolute Convergence
1987-1993	0.052	Absolute Divergence
1993-1999	0.235	Absolute Divergence
1999-2004	-0.018	Absolute Convergence
Pre-1983	0.586	Absolute Divergence
1983-1993	0.025	Absolute Divergence
1993-2004	0.213	Absolute Divergence

The absolute divergence in growth rate of per capita NSDP across states during 1965-72 appropriately substantiates the fact of inter-regional and inter-personal disparities of green revolution. This was largely due to the very limited crop-wise as well as area-wise coverage of the package technology. Therefore some of the states have gained from this 'package technology', but most of the states were lagged behind due to inadequate agricultural infrastructure. Many economists pointed out that the industrial slackness during 1972-83 is due to the overall poor agricultural situations that holding back industrial development 'through the passage of self-limiting nature of unbalanced growth'.[2] Although the period of soft liberalization the per capita across states has shown beta convergence, after economic reforms of 1991 per capita NSDP has shown absolute divergence as evident from the positive coefficients of initial levels of per capita real income for the periods 1987-93 and 1993-99. But, during 1999-2004, the per capita income has again shown convergence. This means that soft reforms have benefited mostly equally all the states which was not happened after 1991.

Mankiw et al. (1992) have used extended neo-classical framework with cross section data to explain region-specific determinants affecting growth. The present study has taken the similar framework of robust, pooled regression to test the convergence hypothesis.

$$\ln (PCNSDP)_{i\,t} = \beta_0 + \beta_1 \ln (PCNSDP)_{i\,t-1} + \Phi X_{it} + \mu_i + \eta_t + e_{it}$$

Here X is exogenously given set of control variables and ì and ç are region-specific and time-specific variables respectively.

Table 3: Pooled Regression with log of PCNSDP as Dependent Variable with State and Time Effect

Independent Variables	Dependent Variable: $ln(PCNSDP)_{it}$					
	Model 1	Model 2	Model 3	Model 4	Model 5	Model 6
Model	Pooled, Robust	Pooled, Robust	Pooled, Robust	Pooled, Robust	Pooled, Robust	Pooled, Robust
State Effect	Yes	Yes	No	No	Yes	Yes
Time Effect	No	No	Yes	Yes	Yes	Yes
$ln(PCNSDP)_{it-1}$	1.170*	0.900*	1.035*	1.029*	0.894*	0.834*
Total Literacy		0.0002		0.0003		-0.005**
Education Expenditure		0.00012*		0.00009 **		0.0002*
Enrolment Ratio		0.002*		0.0004		.0001*
Total Gini		-1.110*		-0.149		-1.186*
F	124.97	147.45	460.83	327.11	128.37	150.33
Adjusted R^2	0.92	0.94	0.94	0.91	0.87	164
Number of Observations	165	164	165	164	165	164
Rate of Convergence / Divergence	1.7%	-1%	3.5%	2.9%	-10.6%	-16.6%

It is seen that after controlling the state specific education variables and disparities, the outcomes of the regression in model six reveals a significant converging trend of growth across the Indian states at approximately 17 percent per annum. By considering only region specific and the time specific effects of heteroscedasticity without controlling the human capital augmenting variables, the states are showing conditional convergence trend of about eleven percent per annum. But when the models are not controlling human capital augmenting variables as well as not manage the either of state or time specific heterogeneity across states, the results reveal diverging trends. The other most important feature is that all the regression outcomes of the present model for lagged log PCNSDP are largely analogous with the previous outcomes. So it is clear from the results that the conditional convergence has been taking place across Indian states during 1960 and 2005, but there is no sign of absolute convergence across states.

As the above model might have a probability that the lagged dependent variable is collinear with the error term, the advanced dynamic GMM (robust) regression would give a solution to remove those problems (Islam, 1995). Following Islam, dynamic panel data model can be framed where difference of log PCNSDP would be regressed on difference of exogenous variables as well as on the difference of lagged dependent variable. The model would be as follows which is free from state specific factors.

$$\Delta \ln (PCNSDP)_{i\,t} = (1 + \beta_1)\, \Delta \ln (PCNSDP)_{i\, t-T} + \Phi\, \Delta X_{it} + \Delta \eta_t + e_{it} - e_{i,\, t-T}$$

Δ is difference and Δ log PCNSDP $_{i\,(t-1)}$ is independent variable and Ä log PCNSDP $_{i(t-2)}$ and further lags are used as instrumental variables.

Table 4: GMM Robust Regression with Instrumental Variables

Independent Variables	Dependent Variable: Δ ln(PCNSDP)$_{i\,t}$		
	Model 1	Model 2	Model 3
Model	GMM, Robust	GMM, Robust	GMM, Robust
Δ ln(PCNSDP)$_{it-1}$	0.914***	1.081	1.099
Δ Totgini$_{it}$	-5.031		
Δ Prim_enrl$_{i\,t}$	0.019	0.018	
Δ Pceduexp$_{it}$	0.001**	0.002**	0.002***
Δ Tot_lit$_{it}$	0 .010	0.025	0.021
Instrumental Variable	Δ ln(PCNSDP)$_{it-2}$ and further lags	Δ ln(PCNSDP)$_{it-2}$ and further lags	Δ ln(PCNSDP)$_{it-2}$ and further lags
F	3.63	3.54	3.47
Number of Observations	133	133	133
Rate of Convergence / Divergence	-8.6%	-8.1%	9.9%

The present outcomes of the GMM regressions have been used to observe the extent of legitimacy of the earlier model observations in a very stringent and critical format. This model has used the first difference of log of PCNSDP by taking into consideration in a dynamic set up to avoid the problem of autocorrelation between the difference in dependent variable and variation in the error term. One important difference of the present model with the earlier ones is that the coefficient on initial output is now 1+ â instead of â in the earlier models.

It has been seen that the conditional convergence has taken place across the Indian states at about eight percent per annum state-specific factors like inequality, literacy, enrolment ratio and education expenditure have been controlled. But when the state specific factors have been withdrawn successively, the states are then diverging. The results are exactly analogous to the previous models, but the rate of convergence or divergence is different. Another important point is that if changes in enrolment ratio and literacy rate can be controlled then conditional convergence across states would prevail.

Findings and Concluding Remarks

It is clear from the results that the coefficients are statistically significant in almost all models although the rate of convergence per year has varied depending on the specifications through the control variables and state and time factors that contingent upon the respective model. However, two important points are to be mentioned. One is that the negative link between inequality and growth in the Indian states during the period of 1960-61 and 2004-05 can be highly explained through the channel of human capital outlays. This means that enhancement of the human capital augmenting variables work positively on growth which makes it possible to achieve conditional â-convergence. Secondly, the effect of inequality on growth is more harmful in the short run to the poorer Indian states that are evident through the positive sign of the interaction variable. This means that with the successive increase in the per capita income of the poorer states in the long run, the intensity of harm may decline, thus implying a more compatible and attuned outcome that Barro has obtained in his study. This finding is identifiable with the conditional convergence in the sense that poor states grow faster through the channel of more accumulation of the human capital.

REFERENCES

1. Barro, R. J. (1991). "Economic Growth in a Cross Section of Countries", Quarterly Journal of Economics, 106(2), pp 407-23.
2. Barro, R. J. and X. Sala-I-Martin (1992). "Convergence", Journal of Political Economy, 100- (2), pp 223-51.
3. Bhattacharya, B. B. and S. Sakthivel (2004). "Regional Growth and Disparity in India", Economic and Political Weekly, 39(10).
4. Bhide, S., R. Chadha and Kaliappa Kalirajan (2005), "Growth Interdependence among Indian States: An Exploration," Asia-Pacific Development Journal, 12-2, pp. 59-80.
5. Cashin, P. and R. Sahay, (1996): "Regional Economic Growth and Convergence in India," Finance and Development, 33, pp. 49-52.
6. Dasgupta, D., P. Maity, R. Mukherjee, S. Sarkar, and S. Chakroborty (2000). "Growth and Inter State Disparities in India", Economic and Political Weekly, 35(27), pp. 2413- 22.
7. Dholakia, R.H. (2003), "Regional Disparity in Economic and Human Development in India", Economic and Political Weekly, 37(39), pp. 4166-72.
8. Ghosh, B., S. Marjit and C. Neogi (1998). "Economic Growth, and Regional Divergence in India: 1960 to 1995", Economic and Political Weekly, 27, pp. 83-116.
9. Islam, N., (1995), "Growth Empirics: A Panel Data Approach," Quarterly Journal of Economics, 110(4), 127-70.
10. Mankiw, N. G., D. Romer and D. N. Weil (1992). "A Contribution to the Empirics of Economic Growth", Quarterly Journal of Economics, 107 (2), pp 407-37.

11. Marjit, S. and S. Mitra (1996), "Convergence in Regional Growth Rates, Indian Research Agenda", Economic and Political Weekly, 31(33), pp. 2239- 42.
12. Patnaik, Prabhat (1972), "Disproportionality Crisis and Cyclical Growth: A Theoretical Note," Economic and Political Weekly, 7 (5-7), pp. 329-336.
13. Persson, T. and G. Tabellini (1994): "Is Inequality Harmful for Growth?" *American Economic Review*, 84, 600-621.
14. Romer, P. M. (1986). "Increasing returns and long run growth", Journal of Political Economy, 94(5), pp. 1002-37.
15. Roy, Hiranmoy and Kaushik Bhattacharjee (2009): "Convergence of Human Development across Indian States", August, *IGIDR Proceedings/Project Reports Series*.
16. Shand, R. and S. Bhide (2000), "Sources of Economic Growth", Economic and Political Weekly, 35 (42).
17. Uzawa, H. (1965): "Optimal Technical Change in an Aggregate Model of Economic Growth", *International Economic Review*, Vol. 6, 18–31.

Data Base:

- Central Statistical Organization (C.S.O), Ministry of Planning, Government of India, New Delhi.
- Data on Education, Education in India, Ministry of Education, Government of India.
- Household Consumer Expenditure in India, 1999-2000, NSSO, *Various Issues*, Government of India.
- National Council of Applied Economic Research, Government of India.
- National Human Development Report of India, 2001, Planning Commission, Government of India, New Delhi
- Selected Educational Statistics, 2000-2001, Budgeted Expenditure on Education, published by D/O Secondary &Higher Education, Government of India.
- www.mopsi.ac.in

NB: The author is greatly indebted to Sugata Marjit and Rajarshi Majumder for many useful suggestions and to the Indian Statistical Institute, Kolkata, NSSO, Kolkata and IEG, New Delhi, for giving the opportunities to obtain valuable dataset to get the perspective of present study. The general disclaimer applies. The author is fully responsible for results and observations used in the present paper.

Footnotes

1. If the coefficient of variation of regional per capita real income will tend to decrease, then it is called sigma (σ) convergence. However, beta-convergence may be obtained without sigma-convergence.
2. See Prabhat Patnaik (1972).

5

Procurement of Tea Labor: A Study on the Dooars Region of Indian Tea Industry

Dr. Nirmal Chandra Roy

ABSTRACT

Tea industry is one of the labour intensive industries and labour is regarded as the heart and soul of this industry. Tea plant needs subtle nuı ture throughout the year. Huge labour is needed for these activities. Indian tea industry offers the second largest employment after the Indian Railway. It requires massive labour at each phase of its exertion right from the cleaning of jungle, nursery preparation, shaping the land appropriate for plantation, draining, and applying manure in the nursery as well as in the plantations for pesticides spraying, plucking, manufacturing, sorting, and then lastly dispatching it to diverse destinations. Devoid of labour, not a single tea plant can survive; as no baby survives without mother.In this paper, an attempted has been drawn up to study the sources of recruitment of tea labour, nature of employment and promotion opportunities of tea labours in the Dooars region of Indian tea industry.

Key Words: *Tea Industry, Labour, Procurement.*

Introduction:

'Tea' the cheapest and widely consumed beverages is regarded as the 'Queen of Beverage' in the world. According to story, teawas revealed in China by the legendary Chinese ruler, ShehNung, in 2737B.C. (Mitra, 2010). The tea industry in Indiatraced back while discovering of homespun tea plant by Robert Bush in Assam in 1823(Banerjee and Banerjee, 2009). According to the Tea Board of India (TBI), India occupies in the second largest position of tea producer which is just after China. India produced 22.68 percent of global production of tea in 2016.India also occupiesthe third largest position as exporter of tea and exported 12.19percent of tea export in the world market by 2016(TBI, 2018).

Indian tea industry gets divided into two distinct parts; the North Indian tea industry and the South Indian tea industry. Out of the entire made tea production in India, the North Indian tea industry produced1093.10 million kilograms by the last year.The total production of West Bengal, which comprises of Terai, Dooars and Darjeeling regionswere 385.87 million kilograms in 2018. The production of made tea in Dooars was 222.63 million kilograms, in Terai the production was 155.52 million kilograms and in Darjeeling hills the production was 7.72 million kilograms. In 2018, the contribution of small tea grower in India was 47.89 per cent (Indian Tea Association, 2019).

Review of Literature:

Several numbers of studies have been conducted on various aspects of Indian tea industry. A notable and relevant research works in connection with the study have been referred below to frame the objectives in the present study.

Bhowmik (1948) in his study focused on the class formation of tribal workers of West Bengal. The study reflected on the migrated workers of outside of Bengal, especially from the Chotonagpur region and their indigenous occupations. Earlier they were agricultural labour and some of them were the poor cultivators. The modes of traditional activities of such labours were changed. Study also reflected that the methods of recruitment, activities and movement of trade unions, social norms of tribes, etc. of those days.

Griffiths (1967) made a laudable work about tea industry of India. In his book, he stated that tea industry of India emerged in early 1830s. This study further revealed that problems of labour in the early stage were prevailed and multifarious problems were also confronted by the planters. The study further elaborately narrated about the labour recruitment, plantation associations, movement of unions, etc. in a lucid manner.

Guha (1977) studied on the two distinct dimensions of tea plantation economy of Assam; the planteraj and the swaraj. The special focus of this study was on the freedom struggle of tea cultivation workers of Assam. The study linked up economic problems and exploitations of tea workers by planters with political development of Assam. The study also dealt with issues such as indentures, agrarian problems, opium, exploitation conducts, etc. of Europian capitalists and planters during the colonial India.

Sarkar (2008) explained about the process of transformation of formal labour market into informal in tea industry of Bengal. In his study, he pointed out that globalization was the main reason for such transformation of labour market. According to the study, due to the global economic changes, tea plantations were not in a suitable position to overcome its costs, especially labour cost. Management of tea estates made strategies of labour flexibility to minimize such costsbut in reality it was not possible because of legislations. Thus, this practice made casual workforces and directly leads to the informal labour market.

Choudhary and Tayal (2010) focused on their study on the permanent labour recruitment by the plantation management. The study was shown that unionization andlabour legislation in tea plantation industry was not functioning in an expected manner for improving the condition of labour. Study further revealed that tea industry of Sri Lanka and India was facing stiff competition from Kenya and China. The study emphasized that improvement of economic and social status of tea workers highly required to combat the competition in international market.

Tamang (2015) made a detail investigation on the historical development of tea cultivation in Dooars and Terai region. The study lighted two aspects; the historical past and present status of the industry. Study reflected that cheap women labour was recruited for the industry. Male labour was recruited specially in the peak season. Earlier, Nepali coolies were involved in cultivation purpose but the number was insufficient and then labours were bought from the adjoining areas through *Sardar*.

From the available literature it has found that not a single study has been conducted on the procurement aspects of labour for theDooars in particular. Thus, the present study is relevant as per the present context.

Objectives of the Study:

The review of literature has impelled in order to frame the following objectives of the study. The central objectives are listed under:

1. A deliberate attempt has beendrawn up to unveilthe sources of recruitment of tea labour in the Dooars region of Indian tea industry.

2. To illuminate the nature employment and promotion opportunities of tea labour in the Indian tea industry of Dooars region.

Methodology for the Study:

The present study is descriptive in nature. The entire

study is based on the secondary data.Secondary data has been gathered from the publications of the Labour Department of Govt. of West Bengal as well as from various tea magazines, master's thesis, doctoral thesis, journal articles, technical reports of various organizations, newspapers, website of Tea Board of India (TBI), website of Indian Tea Association (ITA), books, etc.

Analytical Discussions:

Sources of recruitment of tea labour in the Dooars region

Tea industry is one of the labour oriented industries as it is agro based. It requires massive labour at each phase of its exertion right from the cleaning of jungle, nursery preparation, shaping the land appropriate for plantation, draining, and applying manure in the nursery as well as in the plantation, pesticides spraying, plucking, manufacturing, sorting, and then lastly dispatching it to diverse destinations. Hence, labour is regarded as the heart and soul of tea industry. Devoid of labour, not an individual tea plant can survive; as no baby survives without mother.

In tea industry, labour recruitment system is quite interesting and its history goes long back. During the initial stage of the tea industry in Bengal, labours were recruited from the nearby areas but the numbers were not sufficient. As we know, tea plantations are laying in isolated areas. So, it was not possible by the plantation management to depend only on such labours. Thus, the planters have realized the needs for the alternative sources of labour. Then they started to recruit *'Coolies'*. These *Coolies* were the actual residents of Bihar, Uttar Pradesh, and Odisha. Initially, they were bought by the British for another purpose; to pave the railway track in the northern part of our country. They were called *'Coolies'* because they had to work hard specially lifting heavy weights, cleaning jungles, etc. Their actual livelihoods were the agricultural labour and poor peasant. However, the plantation administration has been identified that on a constant interval, a huge number of the recruited *Coolies* returned back to their respective native place to meet their families and sometimes they never returned to the tea plantation for job. To prevent this practicc, the British planters have realized to settle the family of *Coolies'* to the work place i.e. in the tea plantation area and the other family members of *Coolies'* also were involved in tea plantations. Thus, the family base recruitment system has started in the tea plantations of the Dooars region and till now this system of recruitment of workers prevail.

Nature employment and promotion opportunities of tea labour

In tea plantations, mainly two broad categories of workers are employed: **i)** Permanent worker and **ii)** Casual worker.

i) Permanent Worker: Permanent workers are those residing inside the tea estates and whose names are entered in the estates' workers roll (Register). The position of permanent workers remains same over the years. No new permanent workers position can be created and similarly no such positions can be removed without the approval of appropriate authority. Recruitment process of such positions is family based recruitment i.e. dependent's right. If any worker dies in a particular garden, the legal heir of the deceased person gets job in that position. In addition to this, sometimes permanents workers are recruited through *'Namkati'*. *'Namkati'* is a technical term which means that worker who left the job permanently. In such situations, replacement is made by relatives or dependents of that worker who has left the job. However, in case of the above mentioned two issues, if no dependents or relatives present, recruitment is made in such positions with the consultation of unions.

ii) Casual Worker: Casual worker is technically termed as *'Bigha'* worker. Generally, *Bigha* worker primarily recruited in the peak time of year. Usually, they are recruited during the months of June to September. *Bigha* worker may be available from within the same tea estate or from the outside the tea estate. At the time of recruitment of *Bigha* worker, first precedence is given to the dependents or family members of the permanent worker of the same tea estate. When the number of existing *Bigha* workers is not sufficient, they are recruited from the external sources with consultations of the trade unions.

The process of recruitment of *Bigha* workers from within the tea estate involves a permanent worker (say, husband) whose dependent (wife) would be the *Bigha* worker. He (husband) has to apply to the plantation management. Then the plantation management would ask for medical fitness certificate issued by the Medical Officer of that tea plantation. Then only it may recruit the *Bigha* worker. While recruitment of *Bigha* worker is done from outside the plantations, the common practice is manager or his assistant would observe and ascertain the physical fitness of that person.

Besides the above two categories of workers, *'Thikka'* (contractual) workers are recruited through contractor. In such cases, the entire responsibility regarding recruitment is handed over to the contractor.

The permanent workers are recruited from the dependents or through replacements. Since the number of vacancy for permanent workers remain same over the year, no new position is created. However, the criteria includes for recruitment in such positions, the person should reach at least16 years of age and should have sound health. To be confirmed under this criterion, the person should have to produce medical certificate issued by the Medical Officer (MO) of that tea plantationonly, to the plantation manager.

Promotions of labour to the higher positions of tea gardens are rare in the tea plantations in this region. Only in few tea estates, some labours have been promoted in the higher positions. Those workers were promoted, their position changed to sub-staff and for rare cases staff only. No record exhibits regarding the promotion of worker to managerial potion. So, it may be inferred that promotional opportunity is limited for the tea garden workers in Dooars. However, those were promoted in the staff and sub-staff positions were only male workers. The chance of promotion of male and female workers is not equal to large extent.

Conclusions

From the study, it is concluded that procurement of labour by dependents' right is one of the traditional and conventional recruitment and selection systems by the tea plantations in this region. If, any worker dies in a particular garden, the legal heir of the deceased person gets job in that position. If, no legal heir of that particular worker who has died is present, the management can recruit a new incumbent from within or outside the garden in consultation with the trade unions. Hence, there is limited scope for the external sources of recruitment.As far as promotion of tea labour is concerned, this is observed that there are rare opportunities for the existing workers to get promoted to the higher positions. However, the management of tea plantations of this locale should offer promotion opportunities to the grass root level worker to motivate them for work.

REFERENCES

1. Banerjee, G. and Banerjee, S. (2009). *Tea industry in transition*. New Delhi, India: Abhijit Publications.
2. Bhowmik, S. (1948). *Class formation in the plantation system*. New Delhi, India: People's Publication House.
3. Choudhary, N., &Tayal, D. (2010). A comparative study of the informal condition of the plantation labours of India and Sri Lanka. *The Indian Journal of Labour Economic, 53* (2), 339-357.
4. Griffiths, P. (1967). *The history of the Indian tea industry*. London, England: Weidenfeld and Nicolson.

5. Guha, A. (1977). *Planteraj and swaraj: Freedom struggle and electoral politics in Assam 1820-1947*. New Delhi, India: Delhi University Press.
6. Indian Tea Association, (2019). *Current Tea Scenario*.
7. Retrieve from: https://www.indiatea.org/uploads/scenerio_image/1496839041.pdf(Accessed on 31 of July, 2019)
8. Mitra, D. (2010). *Globalization and industrial relation in tea plantation*. New Delhi, India: Abhijit Publications.
9. Sarkar, K. (2008). Globalization, restructuring and labour flexibility in tea plantations in West Bengal. *The Indian Journal of Labour Economics, 51* (4), 643-654.
10. Tamang, S. (2015). History of tea plantation and its development in Terai-Dooars area of North Bengal: An overview. *Global Journal of Engineering, Science and Social Science Studies, 1*(3), 53-62.
11. Tea Board of India, (2018). *Global Tea*.
12. Retrieve from: http://www.teaboard.gov.in/pdf/Global_Tea_pdf4834.pdf (Accessed on 14th January, 2019)

6

The Malice of Our Society: Human Trafficking

Sandeep Kumar, Vishnupriya & Dr. Dilip Dey

ABSTRACT

The most precious gift given to each and every individual on the planet is the gift of life. Each and every life is significant in its own manner and should be valued. Human beings are the only species on planet that possess intellect. There are two sides of a coin, following it; the use of intellect is dual in nature. The feeling of superiority overrules the emotion of humanity and the being considers other beings of little value and measures them in terms of gain has led to rooting of an inherent evil in our society which is named as HUMAN TRAFFICKING. To begin with, we must know what it actually is. It is the recruitment, transportation, transfer, harboring or receipt of persons, by means of threat or use of force or other forms of coercion, of abduction, of fraud, of deception, of the abuse of power or of a position of vulnerability or of the giving or receiving of payments or benefits to achieve the consent of a person having controlover another person, for the purpose of exploitation. Exploitation shall include, at a minimum, the exploitation of the prostitution of others or other forms of sexual exploitation, forced labor or services, slavery or practices similar to slavery, servitude or the removal, manipulation or implantation of organs. This is an evil beyond measure which needs to be stopped but unfortunate for us, the greed of human beings has blinded them and forced them to conquer actions that are against our morals and the fellow humans become a victim of this gain and the life of an individual serves only as a monetary benefit. The world needs to be free of this malice to sustain as a nurturing environment. Every individual has the power to change the world and we need to take up our responsibility as an individual cell and an organ to eradicate this cancer from the world.

Introduction:

Human trafficking is the trade of humans for the purpose of forced labor, sexual slavery, or commercial sexual exploitation for the trafficker or others. Human trafficking can occur within a country or trans-nationally. Human trafficking is a crime against the person because of the violation of the victim's rights of movement through coercion and because of their commercial exploitation. Human trafficking is the trade in people, especially women and children, and does not necessarily involve the movement of the person from one place to another. According to the International Labor Organization (ILO), forced labor alone (one component of human trafficking) generates an estimated $150 billion in profits per annum. In 2012, the ILO estimated that 21 million victims are trapped in modern-day slavery. Of these, 14.2 million (68%) were exploited for labour, 4.5 million (22%) were sexually exploited, and 2.2 million (10%) were exploited in state-imposed forced labour. Human trafficking is condemned as a violation of human rights by international conventions. The various types of human trafficking are children trafficking, sex trafficking, forced marriage, labour trafficking and trafficking for organ trade. There may be disputes about no mention of various other types of trafficking but they are somehow linked to either one of the types mentioned above, but all in all, each and every type of trafficking begins from the root of considering the life of an individual below others and that is a violation of the laws of humanity that has been implemented upon us for a peaceful environment. The world needs to be free of the evil clutches of trafficking and needs a system of equality to persist throughout the globe to experience the beauty of life.

Literature Review

Human trafficking is a social issue of growing concern across the globe. The estimated number of individuals affected by human trafficking worldwide is 20.9 million people (Hemmings et al., 2016). Human trafficking is defined as, "all acts involved in recruiting, harbouring, transporting, providing, or obtaining a person for compelled service or commercial sex acts through the use of force, fraud, or coercion"(CdeBaca & Sigmon, 2014). While there are various forms of human trafficking that require attention, the focus of this paper will be trafficking for the purposes of sex work. A common factor in human sex trafficking is the movement of victims across borders from poor nations to affluent nations, however domestic human trafficking also exists (Bernat&Winkeller, 2010). Peel Police (2012) stated that over half of the human trafficking cases in Canada have occurred in Peel Region, including both Mississauga and Brampton. There exists minimal evidence-based research on the needs of victims of human trafficking, and the services that are available to them. It is however noted that the health needs of this population are similar to those of other marginalized groups such as migrant labourers, victims of sexual abuse or domestic violence and victims of torture (Williamson, Dutch & Clawson, 2008). Due to the fact that there is little research reported, similar populations can be examined to provide a foundation for the treatment of this population (Williamson et al., 2008). Human Trafficking is acknowledged to be a global human rights violation. Trafficking represents "a denial of the person's rights to liberty, integrity, security and freedom of movement" (GajicVeljanoski& Stewart, 2007).

Framework of Study

Human trafficking is a multidimensional human rights violation that centers on the act of exploitation. Early discussions about trafficking in persons focused almost solely on sex trafficking of women and girls and drew primarily on law enforcement responses. But human trafficking is now understood more broadly to occur in a wide array of low- or no-wage hazardous labor. There is growing evidence on the wide-ranging health consequences of human trafficking. A systematic review on health and human trafficking found that survivors experienced multiple forms of abuse, numerous sector-specific occupational hazards, and dangerous living conditions and suffered a range of poor health consequences. Among trafficking survivors ,nearly half (48%) reported physical or sexual abuse and 22% sustained severe injuries, including lost limbs, and reported symptoms indicative of depression and anxiety disorders. Reports on human trafficking regularly highlight that child workers, minorities, and irregular migrants are at particular risk of more extreme forms of exploitation. Over half of the world's 215 million young workers are estimated to be in hazardous sectors including forced sex work and forced street begging. The terms of employment set the parameters for the ways and extent to which a person can be exploited (e.g., low wages, piecework pay, extended hours, penalties for early termination of contract). After being exploited, many trafficked workers are encumbered by physical and/or psychological health problems and debt. Trafficking victims seldom have access to health or social assistance or legal remedies such as financial compensation for work-related injuries or illness, disability-related lost future earnings, or unpaid wages. Debts and other financial obligations, including for medical care, can increase survivors' vulnerability to further exploitation. Slavery and it's like have existed for millennia; so have social and economic inequalities. Through the declaration of the 2030 Sustainable Development Goals, the international community has promised that efforts will be dedicated to reducing poverty, ensuring healthy lives, and, most encouragingly, promoting decent work. This brings us back to the proposition we posed initially: human trafficking should be considered a global health concern and we need to work together to wipe out this disease from the face of the earth.

Implications:

For too long, the human rights and public health implications of human trafficking have been overlooked, underestimated, and/or misunderstood. Trafficking of humans comprises the recruitment, harboring, and transportation of people for the purpose of exploitation and is considered the world's fastest growing international criminal industry. The trafficking of humans affects approximately 600,000–800,000 men, women, and children around the world. Children can experience extreme forms of exploitation and abuse in the context of human trafficking. Emerging research suggests that 24–56% of trafficked children experience physical violence and 21–51% experience sexual abuse. A large body of evidence from other child populations attests to the adverse effects of physical and sexual violence on children's physical health and wellbeing. Child physical and sexual abuse is also associated with a range of mental disorders, substance abuse, and suicide attempts. **One of the incentives for trafficking is the huge profit made by the buyers and sellers, as well as the criminal organizations that keep the business going. In fact, human trafficking brings in billions of dollars in profit worldwide. The human trafficking needs to be eradicated as soon as possible and a mass awareness is necessary and action is required to overcome this evil and the process has begun long time ago with the hopes of nurturing the fruit of equality in the world.**

Conclusion

The very idea of human trafficking needs to be abhorred as it is thought originating from the trenches of pure evil. The water to the plant of trafficking is the greed of a human being. The need to feel superior and remain superior over others has led to the increase the clutches of the evil which crumples the fellow beings and does not leave any path for them to stand out back. The impact of this act is unimaginable. We ponder over the effects of trafficking at any place where we ourselves are not a part of this vicious circle as a victim. The sheer imagination is not enough to understand the pain because the horrors experienced by the victims are beyond imagination. We as human beings have a moral duty to stop our fellow companions from creating victims and preventing the other fellow companions from becoming victims or else who knows, the next one could be you!

REFERENCES

1. Trafficking in organs, tissues and cells and trafficking in human beings for the purpose of the removal of organs" (PDF). United Nations. 2009. Retrieved 18 January 2014.
2. Convention on Transnational Organized Crime". Unodc.org. Retrieved 22 March 2011.
3. UNODC on human trafficking and migrant smuggling". United Nations Office on Drugs and Crime. 2011. Retrieved 22 March 2011.
4. "A global alliance against forced labour", ILO, 11 May 2005.
5. "What is human-trafficking". Unodc.org. 6 March 2009. Retrieved 21 January 2012.
6. Victims of Trafficking and Violence Protection Act of 2000". State.gov. Archived from the original on 12 March 2009. Retrieved 22 March 2011.
7. Trafficking in Persons Report 2011". U.S. Department of State, 2011.

7

Talent Management Strategies for Attracting and Retaining the Employee in HR Policies

Dr. Soma Mishra

ABSTRACT

There is lack of clarity on the term "talent management" which makes researchers and practitioners left to define the term to suit to it to their requirements. Talent management typically consists of four pillars of intervention viz. attraction, retention, development and deployment. Talent Management according to Lewis and Heckman's (2006) comprises of three different conceptions which are as follows a) a collection of typical human resource department practices, b) the flow of human resources throughout the organization, and thirdly c) sourcing, developing and rewarding employee talent. There have been many practices adopted by different industries in order to manage the talent available with them such as team building, training, identifying talent, talent development, constant feedback etc. Talent management starts with recruitment process, alignment of the workforce to the organization, develop the people and get constant feedback to help in performance of an individual or an organization. The practices adopted generally differ from industry to industry in many cases and certain practices are more suitable for certain industries over others.

Keywords: *Talent Management, Development, Deployment, Rewarding, Attraction, Retention.*

Introduction

Talent management depicts the process through which employers of a wide range of firms, government; non-profits envision their human capital needs and start meeting them. Getting the opportune individuals with the correct skills into the correct jobs, a typical meaning of talent management is the fundamental individual's management challenge in organizations. While the focal point of talent management will in general be on management and official positions, the issues apply to all jobs that are difficult to fill. A fruitful talent management process plans for organizational exchanges. The best method to handle talent management is to utilize a system approach, guaranteeing that the diverse components and bits of the process are working in associate with procure incorporate talent into the system. Human Resource is the sum total of inherent abilities, acquired knowledge and skills represented by the talents and aptitudes of the employees of an organization. Human resources should be utilized to the maximum possible extent in order to achieve individual and organizational goals. An organization's performance and resulting productivity are directly proportional to the quantity and quality of its human resources. That is the reason that the concept of talent management has received a significant degree of professional and academic interest.

Definitions

Talent Management can be defined as the process of recruiting, training, developing, managing, assessing and maintaining an organization's most valuable resource i.e. people.

In this competing marketplace, talent management is one of the most important drivers for organizational success and growth. The organizations must be able to foresee and grab the new opportunities before its competitors. So, in the current scenario, Talent Management has become a new challenge for the next generation "People Managers. It has become extremely important in this competitive market that the organizations should align their talent management initiatives with their business goals. They should also encourage such culture where talented employees are given abundant career development opportunities so that they can perform to the maxinum level. The top management and the HR managers have always been focused on basic Talent Management but to reach the desired levels of success, they require committed, engaged and high-performing employees. It's quite clear that people are an organization's most important assets and as a result, the corporate is adopting different ways to build decision making platforms which are data-driven

Oladapo (2014) stated that when an organization is successful in retaining its top/key talent, it definitely has an impact on the profitability of that organization and he also cited that if the organization is able to manage its talent effectively by having the best talent management practices, it will definitely be beneficial in the long term for the company. He also stated that retaining the employees is dependent on having the best talent management practices and for that the organizations need to have a basic understanding of the concept of talent management.

Sireesha and Ganapavarapu (2014) indicated that talent management is all about getting the right person for the right job at the right place and also at the right time. For this, the organizations need to understand how its employees will behave in future and getting them to behave different from the past to get better results. The ultimate goal of talent management practices or programs implemented by the company must be to get the right people for the right jobs in order to make the company successful but this goal is not that easy to achieve as it sounds.

Sheokand and Verma (2015) found that the talent management concept is emerging slowly in today's business scenario. The human resources also called as the human capital of the organizations serve as the most important component of achieving competitive edge and now, the organizations that function at a global level have started to realize their value and importance.

Organizational Performance

Developing and retaining a workforce which contributes to the performance of the organizations is one of the biggest challenges that the management is facing today. In order to grow and progress in this competitive market, the main goal of every organization is to perform continuously and on a regular basis. So, in order to evaluate the organizations and their actions, organizational performance is the most important criteria. Organizational performance can be defined as a set of financial and non-financial index which provides the information on the level of achievement of its goals and objectives.

The organizational performance is considered to be high when all of its parts function together in order to achieve tremendous results and these results are measured in terms of the value that it creates and delivers to its clients or customers. Every organization needs talented employees to increase the productivity and maximize the overall organizational performance. It is possible for organizations to gain a sustainable competitive advantage over its competitors only when its human resources are innovative and creative. When the entire global market is assessed, it is seen that companies achieve the top position in their market and produce perfect business outcomes if they give priority to develop themselves, their people and deliver differentiated products and services to their customers. So, in order to do so, organizations must identify the talents, assess their potentials and develop their skills and abilities accordingly.

There are some factors which are identified by the researchers which contribute towards the performance of the organizations:

- **Continuous learning:** The organizations need to develop certain systems which help its employees to learn, learn and learn. Such a culture greatly helps the organizations to become high performers in the industry.
- **Focusing on the customer results/outcomes:** The organizations need to focus on the value which they create for its customers. If the customers are satisfied, then, automatically the revenues and the organizational performance go up.
- **Aligning systems and structures:** If the organizations want to perform better, then, they need to align their systems, structures and all the processes with the business goals and strategies and also need to go along with its vision and mission.
- **Employee involvement:** The organizations should work towards creating high involvement of its employees. It can do so by giving autonomy to its talented employees so that they are to make their own decisions, respecting their creativity and unique ideas and also by encouraging them to perform better.
- **Information sharing:** There should be an open communication in the organization and there is should be a free flow of the information as well. Employees should be informed about all the changes made and decisions taken and this would help the organization to perform better.

The organizational performance can be measured in both the financial as well as the financial terms. The financial measures that show whether the organization is performing well or not are the return on investments, high revenues, sales growth and high market share. On the other hand, the non-financial measures of organizational performance are the satisfaction of employees, customer satisfaction, less complaints, good relationship with the suppliers and also the trust of the employees in the leadership. If the organization is performing well in both these areas, then, it can be termed as a high performing organization. To drive this high performance, the involvement of the talented workforce is needed because they are the core competencies and assets which a company has. This human or intellectual capital of the organization helps it to achieve its goals and objectives and also to generate above average returns and excellence as well.

Talent management differs from previous HR processes for hiring, training, and retaining employees and indeed from HR itself in several key ways:

- Where hiring, training, and retention before were centralized in the HR department, with talent management many of these duties are federated to the front-line managers actually leading the employees in question. In this way, the whole organization is responsible for, and has a stake in these activities.
- HR is more administrative-focused, dealing with pay, vacation days, benefits, and complaints, while talent management is almost singularly-focused on helping and improving the top talent in the organization. Think professional development vs. tracking attendance.
- Talent management is strategic, often manifesting as a company-wide long-term plan closely associated with overall business goals, while HR is more tactical, dealing with the day-to-day management of people.

Human Resources and Talent Management

- Human resources have a compelling mission to provide value added services; however, this expectation is often hard to describe. Further, HR leaders are asked to provide line of sight plans that support institutional strategy and challenges; again, not an intuitive task. It is, perhaps, more clarifying to examine effective, leading-edge practices that have been or could be put in place that deliver on the promise of excellence in human resource management. Here, some successful strategies are examined in the areas of talent retention, growth and employee engagement.

- HR's responsibility related to talent management is to identify investments, design development required to fully deliver on its role in TM, and calculate the return on investment to the organization. HR should assess the ability of the organization's decentralized leadership to implement local or unit-based actions required to close identified talent gaps. Assume that one initiative will be to retain high performers in strategic and core roles. A decision model may assist both central HR and local leadership to identify actions appropriate to different performance segments.
- This decision model is sometimes referred to as the "Can Do/Will Do Matrix". The model identifies performance quadrants and HR or local leadership talent management initiatives to address each subgroup. The vertical axis represents ability, or «can do»; the horizontal axis represents willingness to contribute, or «will do». In each quadrant, HR should plan with local leadership how to address and resolve issues of accountability, engagement, competency development, growth and reward.

Talent Management Process

Organizations are made up of people: people creating value through proven business processes, innovation, customer service, sales, and many other important activities. As an organization strives to meet its business goals, it must make sure that it has a continuous and integrated process for recruiting, training, managing, supporting, and compensating these people. The following steps show the complete process:

Step: 1 Workforce Planning

- The key of talent management begins with talent searching and recognizing individuals for their unique strengths. Planning consist of the process of knowing how to select appropriate individuals as employees based on their skills, knowledge, pragmatism, maturity and making sure that they are smoothly fitted into their assigned roles as well as the overall system. Planning further refer to using the available assets for the effective implementation of the production plan.

Step: 2 Recruiting

- The recruitment and selection activities are the major functions of the HR department as they create the competitive strength of the company. The company has to decide the position to be filled through manpower planning, carrying job analysis, developing the job description, and job specification, followed by the finalizing the man specification. Through an integrated process of recruiting, assessment, evaluation, and hiring the business brings people into the organization.

Step: 3 Onboarding

- The organization must train and enable employees to become productive and integrated into the company more quickly. A carefully designed placement system improves employee morale, which in turn reduces employee turnover and absenteeism.

Step: 4 Performance Management

- Performance management is the means through which managers ensure that employees' activities and output are congruent with the organizational goal. It is central to gaining competitive advantage, and comprises three phases- defining performance, measuring performance, and taking a feedback on the performance.

Step 5: Training and Performance Support

- Training is an HRD mechanism that improves the knowledge, skills and the performance of the employee. Most of the organizations identify specific training needs prior to training its people. Once the training needs are identified, development of the training objectives should be carried out. Trained and developed talents have a greater probability of staying and growing in a company.

Step 6: Succession Planning

- Investment in human capital requires careful planning. Under the talent management umbrella, succession planning and leadership development are important organizational business strategies to develop and retain talent. As the organization evolves and changes, there is a continuous need to move people into new positions. Succession planning, a very important function, enables managers and individuals to identify the right candidates for a position. This function also must be aligned with the business plan to understand and meet requirements for key positions 3-5 years out. While this is often a process reserved for managers and executives, it is more commonly applied across the organization.

Step 7: Compensation and Benefits

- Compensation management is a strategic issue and

includes all forms of pay and rewards given to employees. A sound and effective compensation system is the key driver of motivation, employee retention, and enhanced quality of work life. Many organizations try to tie the compensation plan directly to performance management so that compensation, incentives, and benefits align with business goals and business execution.

Step 8: Critical Skills Gap Analysis

- This is a process we identify as an important, often overlooked function in many industries and organizations. While often done on a project basis, it can be "business-critical." For example, today industries like the Federal Government, Utilities, Telecommunications, and Energy are facing large populations which are retiring. How do we identify the roles, individuals, and competencies which are leaving? What should we do to fill these gaps? We call this "critical talent management" and many organizations are going through this now.

Evolution of Talent Management

- Evolution of Talent Management may be tracked way back in the 1980s and 1990s organizations realized that the HR function was in fact more important - and the concepts of "Strategic HR" emerged. During this period organizations realized that the VP of HR had a much larger role: recruiting the right people, training them, helping the business design job roles and organization structures (organization design), develop "total compensation" packages which include benefits, stock options and bonuses, and serving as a central point of communication for employee health and happiness.
- The "Head of Personnel" became the "VP of HR" and had a much more important role in business

strategy and execution. The systems which were built up to support this new role include recruiting & applicant tracking (ATS), portals, total compensation systems, and learning management systems. In this role, the HR department now became more than a business function: it is a business partner, reaching out to support lines of business.

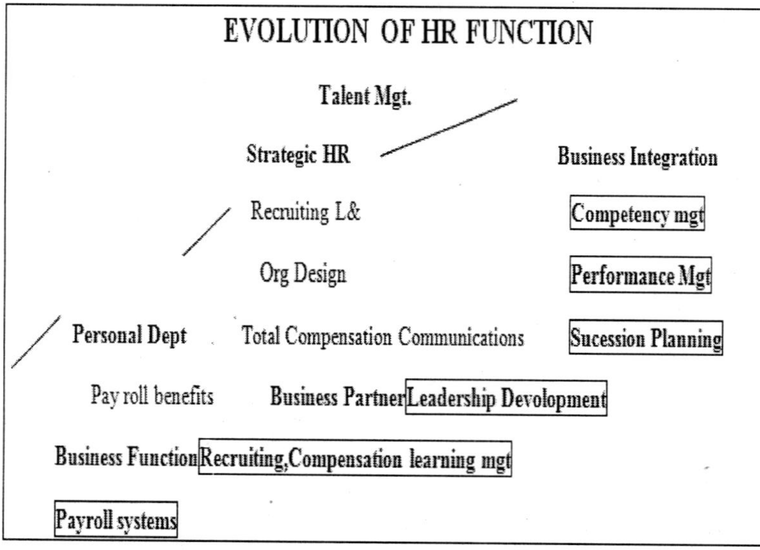

Conclusion:

The study concluded that the organization ensures that the competencies identified for individual employees match the goals and objectives of the organization and is focused on developing its employee's careers in line with its goals. The study also concluded that the organization has been successful in building a sustainable management employer brand and makes executives the primary Talent managers. Finally, the study concluded that talent management strategies are the greatest enablers of organization for attracting and retaining the employees in HR policies.

REFERENCES

1. Abraham, S. (2011). *Talent Management Strategies of an International Bank in the Middle-East*, 608-617.

2. Axelrod, B., Handfield-Jones, H. and Michaels, E. (2002), "A new game plan for C players", *Harvard Business Review*, 80(1), pp. 80-8.

3. Balachandran, S. M.; Mishra, S. A. K.&Chaudhury, S. R. K. (2010)*Talent management in the Indian banking system*, pp. 1-3.

4. Bartel, A.P. (1994), 'Productivity Gains from the Implementation of Employee Training Programs', *Industrial Relations*, 33(1) pp.411-425.

5. Bassett, P.; Buxton, C.; Pathania, R. &Sharan, M. (2007). *Talent Management Is Key to India's Pharma Future*, pp. 1-4.

6. Bauer, T. N. (2007). *On boarding New Employees: Maximizing Success*. SHRM Foundation's Effective Practice Guidelines Series. Retrieved from www.shrm.org/foundation.

7. Berger, L.A. & Berger, D.R. (2003). *The Talent Management Handbook: Creating Organizational Excellence by Identifying, Developing and Promoting Your Best People*, McGraw-Hill, New York.

8

A Study on the Impact of Digitization on Employment in India

Ipsita Paria

ABSTRACT

Digitization in India had been launched around 1980s when first computer had been introduced in country. Since that time digitization in various industries had been evolved and it had a huge impact on the employment scenario of the country. The main objective of this study is to find out the impact of digitization on employment status in India, changing scenario of job profile among industries in the country. Various researchersacross India made various researches to find out the status of employment across industries in the country and made conclusion witn the outcome of research to show the scenario of employment market of India post digitization.

Keywords: *Digitization, Employment market*

Introduction

Digitization is to convert analog signals to digital form. In this way we are able to perform manual and paper-based work digitally. Digital automation process helps to reduce redundancy, error rate, process time etc.So, digitization improves the operational process by avoiding human made manual error. On the other side artificial intelligence has successfully analyzed the normal trend of business and customer preference by surveying their frequently used data. In this scenario question is arising about the relationship between digitization and its impact upon present job market of the country. If all operational activities can be done through online mode then it will be having a huge impact on labour market of the country. Now the study will focus to find out is digitization really cut down the job market or only fact is that some traditional job will obsolete and new job profile will be created in future. This review paper will try to draw a conclusion about the mentioned fact by analyzing various research paper and journal article and company survey [1][2].

Objectives of Literature review

Prime objectives of this literature review are as mentioned below:

- To understand the various thoughts, studies, analysis that is made by various researchers and authors till date to conclude is digitization is helpful to growth of employment in country.
- To understand the fact that digitization is how much impactful on the job opportunity of the country

Review of Literature on the studies that satisfy the stated objectives of the Paper:

In 2013, Karim Sabbagh, Roman Friedrich, Bahjat El-Darwiche, Milind Singh, Alex Koster conducted a study for The Global Information Technology Report where they tried to find out How digitization works for economic growth and job creation on both industry as well as regional perspective. In this research it was found that Job creation in emerging economy region like India is much higher side than advanced economic region. They concluded that digitalization can lead to productivity boost of the country which will improve the economy and labour market of the country [3]. In 2015, Saima Khan, Dr. Shazia Khan &MohsinaAftab conducted a study that how digitization is impactful on Indian Economy. With advanced technology it creates a great impact on economy especially on labour market. It has huge opportunity in IT sector, software development, outsourcing etc. Author concluded that though digitization is required for hassle free work but original knowledge is important in respect artificial knowledge as digital performance always require maintenance and up gradation [4]. In 2017 ShravanNune in his article analyzed how automation is being impactful on Indian employment opportunity. Automation becomes a major reason for job cut among various industry. But this scenario can be changed if proper strategy can be taken like skill upgradation of employees, flexible labour law, and proper employee protection etc.[5]. In 2018, International Labour Organization made a research on new technologies in India and how it will affect future job market of India. India is facing issue of unskilled or semiskilled employee in every industry who are having lack of knowledge of digital platform. So there will be a huge gap for skilled employees which lead to employment opportunity in the country. They concluded that Job opportunities can only be restricted as education level and skill are low among labours[6]. In 2018, Ganesh Natarajan narrated in his article new skills will increase job opportunity and as well as entrepreneur opportunity for youth. If digitization can be deployed at every stage of livelihood creation then this will create a huge job opportunity for youth. Skill identification and properly skilled manpower is required to retain old jobs as well as find new jobs in era of digitization [7]. In an article of Silicon India, Sanjay Sinha and Dr. Saritprava Das explained that how digitization across industries will create more and better jobs for country.Huge growth has been witnessed in financial market, agriculture, real estate; Service industry etc so computer literate individual is required.As per author, employment will be created as a part of digital development in the country [8]. In 2018, Terri Chapman, Samir Saran, Rakesh Sinha, Suchi Kedia, Sriram Gutta has made an survey for World Economic forum to show the future employment status of India. Future employment status is uncertain but there is huge opportunity if digitization can be implemented properly. The authors concluded that technological disruption can only managed by skilled human being which leads to employment opportunity in digital India [9].

Implications of the study

Main focus of the study is to understand how employment of Indian industry has been affected with the introduction of digitization in each sector. Initially India has been affected by this digitization as different types of present job profile have going to be obsolete as manpower have been replaced by the automated service. But soon new job profiles have been created which still does not exist. The impact of digitization on different domains in India might be expressed depending upon different analysis.

Impact on GDP per capita

Different analysis reveals that 10% increase of country's digitization may fuels a growth of its GDP per capita by 0.75 percent for that country.

Impact on unemployment

Digitization creates more jobs rather it has destroyed;similarly, analysis reveals that 10% increase of country's digitization will reduce the unemployment rate by 1.02 percent.

The present study will be helpful for shaping future job industry as well as to understand the future view of the employers about recruitment where most of them speak about increase of net employment gain so far.Impact of Digitization on sector wise employment is discussed in the next section.

Financial Sector: In India, Digital transactions were only just 8%, As a result of digitization; it is expected to go up to 36% by 2027. All the financial institutions like banks, share trading companies have implemented online platform for financial transactions using different APPs, internet banking etc. Huge amount of jobs has been created for implementing and maintaining technological approaches in financial sectors.

Retail Sector: Retail sector is expected to grow to US $ 1.3 trillion by 2020. Numbers of online retailer are increasing with the time. Huge jobs are created in these sectors for vendor tie-up, logistics, warehouse maintenances, distribution of sold products. As per the technological view new jobs also has been created for website implementation and maintenance, server maintenance and promoting of retailer site.

Technology Sector: India remained the world's top sourcing destination in 2016-17 with a share of 55 per cent. Indian IT &ITeS companies have set up over 1,000 global delivery centers in over 200 cities around the world. As digitization increases the numbers of new companies which do their business in online mode, So a huge numbers of online application, database servers, network have been implemented and their maintenance have to be provided. Thus creates a huge amount of jobs. Rather than thesenew jobs are created for digital marketing, online product promotion, customer behavior analysis.

Healthcare Sector: Healthcare sector is going to be one of the largest sectors in respect of employment which is increasing at 15%. The volume was US $ 158.2 billion in 2017. As impact of digitization, a healthcare service (like booking appointment, patient medical history, doctor consultant) has been provided in online mode. Thus huge jobs are created in this sector.

Education Sector: India has more than 1.5 million schools, 751 universities and 35,539 colleges. India is the second largest market for e-learning with a market volume of around US $ 5.7 billion by 2020. Different online mode degrees, online learning APPS, online classroom coaching, online study material has been designed with the help of digitization. Huge amount of jobs are created for development and maintenance of online platforms for education as well as for online tutors.

Media and Entertainment Industry: The volume of the television sector is US$ 15.2 billion in 2019 with a growth rate of 15.5 percent. Digitization has provided the opportunity to grow this sector by providing the access of Radio, television, music and entertainment in user mobile phone with the help of cheap internet.Huge jobs are created for online content making, digital promotion, digital advertisement and digital marketing.

Service sector: With the help of digitization, different services like legal document processing, online proof checking, online editing, call centers, online data entry, online data processing, online marketing, online surveys etc. have been provided to the online users. Thus high volume of jobs has been created from these sectors.

Conclusion

Various researcher and Author shared their opinion about the impact of digitization on job opportunity in their research, study and analysis. It is true that digitization is one of the cause of unemployment as human repetitive jobs are now done with the help of technology like artificial intelligence, automation etc. But this can be taken care by proper skill upgradation which is required for new job profile. Government will also play an important role as they will be responsible for employee protection through smooth job transition of the employees. So we can conclude that though old job profiles are going to obsolete in near future in era of digitization but it will not affect employment market of the country because new job profiles will also be created according to the situation demands.

REFERENCES

1. https://en.wikipedia.org/wiki/Technological_unemployment
2. https://www.indiatoday.in/magazine/cover-story/story/20160502-employment-sc
3. http://www3.weforum.org/docs/GITR/2013/GITR_Chapter1.2_2013.pdf
4. Khan, S.; Khan, S.&Aftab, M. (2015)."Digitization and its impact on Economy", "International Journal of Digital Library Services".1(2): 138-49. ISSN: 2250-1142 (Online), ISSN 2349-302X (Print).
5. https://www.jagranjosh.com/current-affairs/impact-of-automation-on-employment-opportunities-analysis-1507117867-1
6. https://www.ilo.org/wcmsp5/groups/public/—asia/—ro-bangkok/—sro-new_delhi/documents/publication/wcms_631296.pdf
7. https://www.rediff.com/business/column/can-digital-india-create-more-jobs-than-it
8. https://education.siliconindia.com/viewpoint/digitizing-industry-a-way-to-create-more—better-jobs-in-india-nwid-10759.html
9. https://www.orfonline.org/wp-content/uploads/2018/10/Future-of-Work-in-India_Re

9

Murshidabad, a District of West Bengal (India): An Introduction of Tourism Management Perspective

Dr. Mustak Ahmed

ABSTRACT

Murshidabad is one of the important districts in respect to tourism in the state West Bengal of the country India. This district is directly associated with British and Mughal history. There are so many heritage architectures of those periods, which are the attractions of domestic as well as international tourists. It is one of the socio economically backward districts of West Bengal. Now by the help of the government and some nongovernmental organisations the district's socio-economic scenario is changing. As a result, the tourism sectors are also developing gradually. Though, the potentialities are not utilised properly as it consisted. If we be able to take care for development and promotion the tourism resources of the district then, every sides of the socio-economic development are possible of the concerned peoples. This paper has covered to identify the tourism potentialities, tourism products, tourism opportunities and threats.

Key-Words: *Tourism in Murshidabad, Tourism Potentialities, Opportunities and Challenges, Socio-economic development*

Introduction

Murshidabad was the last capital city of independent Bengal before British rule was named after NawabMurshidQuli Khan,Dewan of Bengal, Bihar and Odisha and situated on the banks of the Bhagirathi River. It was made the capital of undivided Bengal in 1717. The British shifted the capital to Kolkata in 1773. Plassey (Palashi), where the historic battle was fought in 1757 between NawabSiraj-ud-Doula and Lord Clive of the East India Company, is only 40 km south of Hazarduari, Murshidabad. Source: Department of Tourism Website Government of West Bengal.

Murshidabad is a unique district of the state West Bengal for its natural beauty and for lush green countryside. This district is famous for varioustypes of testy mangoes. There are many big mango gardens in the north part of this district.From the Nawabs of the pre-British era to the Lords from England, Murshidabad has seen history from its core. This small tourist haven in West Bengal serves as a place that manages to combine the beauty of the past with the beliefs of the present.Calling it a religious town or a monument city would mean limiting its beauty and restricting it magnificence. This town reminds the tourists that no matter how forward technology has brought us, some things are best experienced on foot. The city will transport the tourists to a beautiful, ancient time and give the tourists a great sense of peace and satisfaction.

Objectives of the Study

The major objectives of the study are mentioned below.

- To identify the tourism products in Murshidabad district.
- To measure tourism potentialities in Murshidabad district.
- To study the impact of tourism on concerned people of this district.

➢ To study the opportunities and challenges of tourism of Murshidabad.

Literature Review

Tourism is primarily about human activity which involves travel from an originating area to a destination for pleasure or business purposes. The concept embraces cultural, economic and social exchange processes. These elements are inextricably bound together in mesh of activity which we refer to travel and tourism. Furthermore, writers often refer to tourism within the context of an origin-destination matrix. Pearce, for example, in referring to Thurot's multiple origin-destination model comments: Tourism is thus a multi-faceted activity and geographically complex one as different serviceis sought and supplied at different stages from the origin to destination. Moreover, in any country or region there is likely to be a number of origins and destinations, with most places having both generating (origin) and receiving (destination) functions. (Pearce, 1989, p.2)

Tourism usually is defined as a form of recreation that takes place beyond a specified distance from the permanent home or place of job. Since 1970s, the term 'tourism' has been commonly used to describe the field of travel and reflected to some extent the increasing growth in pleasure travellers, who were generally called tourists or travellers. Tourism has wider implications encompassing for economic benefits and socio-cultural benefits as well to the concerned societies. According to Professor Hunziker and Krapf in the year 1942, gave a technical definition of tourism as "Tourism is totality of the relationship and phenomenon arising from the travel and stay of strangers, provided the stay does not imply the establishment of a permanent residence and is not connected with a remunerated activity." The Tourism Society in Britain had also attempted to clarify the concept and in the year 1976 defined it as "Tourism is the temporary short-term movement of people to destinations; outside the places where they normally live and work and their activities during the stay at these destinations it includes movement for all purposes, as well as day visits or excursions." According to Mathieson and Wall (1982), "Tourism is the temporary movement of people to destinations out of their normal home and work place, the activities undertaken during the stay, and the facilities created to cater for their needs." Tourism is currently the largest and the fastest growing industry in the world. Tourism is today most attractive and resourceful multi-billion industries in India. Today tourism is highlighted for its immense business scope. Tourism is not an activity for pastime and entertainment but is an enriching activity. In 19th century travel for recreation was only undertaken by the elite society. Then the scenario is changing gradually. And by 21st century, travel became a new concept of economy-tourism available to all with huge money.Tourism industry is existed at the second largest industry in revenue-generating just next to the oil industry.The direct contribution of Travel & Tourism industries to the world gross domestic product (GDP) and employment in 2015 was US$ 2.20 trillion and 108.0 million concerned jobs respectively. By taking its vast impacts, including indirect and induced contributions, into account, total contribution of Travel and Tourism to the global economy in the year 2015 was US$ 7.20 trillion (2015 prices) and which equates to 9.80% of the total GDP. In terms of employment, in the year 2015 the Travel and Tourism sector providing directly and indirectly around 284 million jobs that is 1 in 11 of all jobs in the whole world. 2.50 million New jobs were generated directly in the sector in the year 2015, by taking the number of direct jobs to 108 million. In total, 7.20 million new jobs were generated as a result of direct and indirect and also by induced activities. The total contribution of Travel and Tourism industry for employment grew by 2.60 % in the year 2015, while the total GDP contribution grew by 3.10 % which is faster than wider economic growth (2.30%) for the few consecutive years. In employment growth terms of the Travel and Tourism sector outperformed various other select industries in the year 2015 including the financial services, health care and education sectors. Source: WTTC, Travel & Tourism Economic Impact 2016 (Annual Update Summary).

Tourism in West Bengal:

The state, West Bengal is a unique state in India in terms of travel and tourism. It has all the three vital ingredients of tourism; those are sea, mountains and forest. At the time of partition in 1947, Bengal was split into East Bengal(presently Bangladesh) and West Bengal. The Bangladesh is an independent country while West Bengal became a state of the Indian republic with Kolkata as its capital. Geographically this state West Bengal is comparatively long and narrow and running from theGange's delta in the south to the Himalayas with Darjeeling. West Bengal is a state in Eastern India that abounds bounties of lush green village side. West Bengal has the widest variety of attractions in terms of tourist spots from the bustling Kolkata mega polis with its historical and modern charms, to the zones of tranquillity like the Himalayan terrain in the far north to the Sundarbans forest of Mangrove trees in the far south. From the Chotonagpur plateau region in the West, forests in the north and south-west, mountains Himalaya in the north and sea beaches of the Bay of Bengal in the south.More specifically it is stated, the Himalayas capped with white snow, Darjeeling, referred by many as the Queen of the Hill Stations and the Himalayan Railway in Darjeeling has been declared as a World Heritage site by the UNESCO, the vast tea estates in the Dooars region, the famed Royal Bengal Tiger of Sundarban, the innumerable historical landmarks of India and as well as of Bengal glorious and enriched history are all wonders for the prospective domestic as well as international tourists. The Government of West Bengal has realized the huge potential of tourism industry in this part and hence has formulated an appropriate policy framework to attract more domestic and international tourists. West Bengal is one of the most culturally and ethnically unique and famous states of India.

This state occupies 4 % of the total area where live almost 8 % of the total population. In the year 2015, total 80,27,133 Foreign Tourists Arrived in India, out of which 14,89,500 visited to West Bengal. No. of foreign tourist arrivals in India is 7.68 million and annual growth rate is 10.20 percent. Foreign earning from tourism is in INR terms 123,320 crore and US $ terms US$ 20.24 billion and annual growth rate is 14.5 percent. West Bengal has experienced an increase of 5.30 % in tourist arrivals since the year 2014. The foreign tourist in West Bengal grew by 2% and domestic tourist rose by 12% in the year 2013 over the previous year's figures. Foreign Tourist Arrivals (FTAs) in this state is 1375740 and 1489500 in the year 2014 and 2015 respectively and where 49029590 and 70193450 were the Domestic Tourist Visit in 2014 and 2015 respectively.Source: Annual Report 2015-16, Tourism Finance Corporation of India Limited.

Foreign tourist and domestic tourist visits in the state West Bengal

Year	*Foreign Tourists (in Lakh)*	*Domestic Tourists (in Lakh)*
2010	11.9	211
2011	12.1	222
2012	12.2	227
2013	12.5	255
2014	13.7	490
2015	14.9	702
2016	15.2	744
2017	15.7	796

Source: "India Tourism Statistics", Ministry of Tourism and State/ Union Territory Tourism Departments.

The state West Bengal aims to become a preferred tourism and tourism-related investment destination for the investors in the country for its unique geographical characteristics along with its various tourism-related interests. The tourism industry in West Bengal has become one of the most efficient earning avenues for the state and concerned local people. West Bengal is an important province in respect to tourism in India. Tourism is the right vehicle for developing a state like West Bengal which is on the path of modern economic growth. The value added effect of tourism is increasing the quality of tourism industry in West Bengal.West Bengal is having geographically unique characteristics in respect to other states of India for sharing its international boundary with the countries of Nepal, Bhutan and Bangladesh and domestically with the states, Jharkhand, Bihar, Orissa and Assam. The state is having the unique characteristics for the connection with the frozen Himalaya in the far North and the attractive coastal line in the far South of the state. The state is having 5 national parks, 15 wildlife sanctuaries, and 3 tiger reserve forests. Over the past decade mass tourism in various conventional forms occupied the tourism market in West Bengal, but by the changing scenario of purchasing habit of the tourist (customer), the attention is shifting gradually to the new tourism products like, rural tourism, eco-tourism, agri-tourism, wild life tourism etc. Presently the government of West Bengal recognising the tourism industry as one of the massive potential and has drawn up ambitious plan to develop it.

Murshidabad at a glance from Tourism Perspective

Geography

The District of Murshidabad has an area of 2143 sq. m.(or 5316.11 sq. km). In shape, the district resembles an isosceles triangle with its apex pointing to the North-West. Murshidabad is in the middle of West Bengal lying between 23°43′N and 24°52′N latitude and 87°49′E and 88°44′E longitude with district head quarter at Baharampur. The Padma River flows through the entire Eastern boundary, separating the district from the districts of Malda and Rajshahi (Bangladesh). Burdwan and Nadia are in the Southern side and Birbhum and the Pakur(Jharkhand) are on the Western side of the district. The main river Bhagirathi divides it into two almost equal portions the district namely 'BAGRI' on eastern side and 'RARH' on western side.

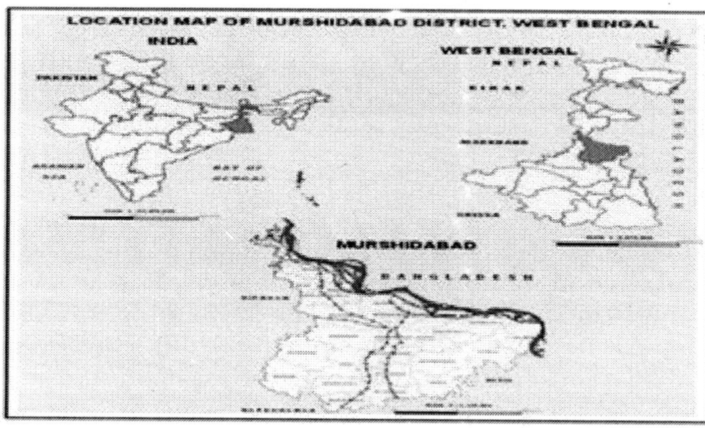

Murshidabad is located at the north-eastern boundary of the Presidency division.The district has an international border with Bangladesh covering a distance of 125.35 km of which 42.35 km. is on land and the remaining is riverside running along 11 blocks. Murshidabad has 254 Gram Panchayyats, 26 blocks, 5 Sub-divisions and 7 Municipalities. Source: murshidabad.gov.in

Demography

Total Population of Murshidabad district is (as per Census 2011) 71,02,430. Out of which Bengali Muslims is 75.09% forms the majority of population while Bengali Hindus forms 23.89%. Murshidabad district has 6% of the area and comprises 7.78% of the total population of West Bengal. As per Census 2011, the total population is 71.02 lakh and is expected to cross 70 lakh and the literacy rate is 63.88%. Murshidabad has a large concentration of minority population may be more than 66% of the total population. It is educationally backward and the poor female literacy rate is a matter of concern.

Religion	*Percentage (%)*
Muslim	75.09
Hindu	23.89
Christians	0.04
Sikhs	0.04
Others	0.94

Total Population (as per Census 2011)	71,02,430
Male	36,29,595
Female	34,72,835
Decadal growth	21.07%
Sex Ratio	957
Population density	1334/sq. Km.
Literacy rate (as per Census 2011)	63.88%
Male	61.25%
Female	55.04%
Child sex ratio	963
Rural population (%)	80.22%
Urban population (%)	19.78%

Source: murshidabad.gov.in

History

The district derives its name from Murshidabad. The Mughal emperor Aurangzeeb sent his Diwan, Kartalab Khan toMurshidabadregion for collection of revenue during his regime. The emperor (Aurangzeeb) became very pleased with Kartalab Khan (Diwan) for his activities and performance and for that named him (Kartalab Khan) as MurshidKuli Khan. MurshidKuli Khan shifted the provincial revenue headquarter (H.Q) from Dacca (presently in Bangladesh) to Murshidabad in 1704 (A.D). The name 'Murshidabad' comes from the place known as "Muksudabad" which was the capital of Bengal during Murshid Quli Khan's rule. Before the advent of British, the city of Murshidabad was the capital of undivided Bengal. Since the time of Nawab Murshid Kuli Khan (1704-1725 A.D) to last Nawab Mirjafar (1757 to 1760 A.D) many beautiful artistic creations, sculptures, palace buildings, mosque, temples etc. have been built which attract the foreign and domestic tourists all over the year.It has a great significance in the Indian History as in 1757 the British defeated Siraj–ud–Daula in the Battle of Plassey, after which the entire nation was brought under the British Colonial Rule. The Murshidabad town still bears many memories of the Nawabs with tombs, mosquesand gardens and retains such industries as carving in ivory, gold and silver embroidery and silk weaving etc. British lord, Warren Hastings removed the supreme civil and criminal courts to Calcutta in 1772, but in 1775 the latter courts were brought back again to Murshidabad. In 1790, under British Lord Cornwallis, the entire revenue and judicial staffs were moved to Calcutta. The Hazarduari Palace, dating back to 1837, is a magnificent building. It (Murshidabad) was constituted as a municipality in 1869 and it remains to the present day.The city is also famous for producing exotic mangoes and litchis.

Shopping

Murshidabad is a place of historic interest. Silk of Murshidabad, products of Belmetal and Solacrafts of this district are very much popular in inland as well as export market. Murshidabad is famous for handicrafts (ivory and wood) products. Ivory carving has been patronized from the Nawabs time and about 99% of total production of ivory is exported, which draws a significant amount of Murshidabad`s income. Bamboo and clay handicrafts are also produced by the local skilled artisans and sell to the domestics as well as foreign tourists.

Sandalwood etching has become more popular than ivory carving now. This district is also famous for brass metal and bell metal. Murshidabad silk sarees are famous all over the world. Kora Saree is a very popular variety of sarees. These sarees are famous all over the country and even the world for their intricate designs and pattern works.

Murshidabad District Museum

Late Rai Bahadur Surendra Narayan Singha of Jiaganj was the initiator and founder, who had contributed everything contained therein. The land of the Museum and the invaluable sculptures and others antiquities (items) are entirely from his contributions and collections. The Museum is located at Nahalia, Jiagunj just beside the palace of Late Rai Bahadur about 2km. away from Jiaganj Railway Station. Rai Bahadur collected a large numbers of stone sculptures from different parts of the country, especially from erstwhile Bengal and Bihar. He donated all items to the Government of West Bengal in 1962. The construction of the Museum building was started by the state government in 1965 over the donated landand the construction completed in 1985. The museum showcases largely of his personal collections, Manuscripts (on Ayurveda, Tantra, and theRamayana) and also some rare books. A nominal entry fee of Rs. 5 is collected from the visitors and photography is strictly prohibited inside the museum.At present there are three full-fledged galleries. Those sculptures and different art objects are displayed in those galleries through wall showcases and pedestals. There are some marvellous masterpieces recovered from recent archaeological excavations in different sites in this district have also been displayed in the museum.

Local food and cuisine

Murshidabad is not particularly famous for any special cuisine, but numerous good hotels have decent eating places where the tourists can enjoy a nice meal.

Murshidabad is also known for 'murgi biryani', gobindabhoghchal (rice) and misti (sweet) polaow among a host of other Bengali and Muglai dishes.

Bera Utsav

The grand celebrations of 'Bera Utsav' are conducted at Lalbagh, on the banks of the river Bhagirathi (Ganga), very near the palace of Nawabs. The attractive celebration is adorned by traditional dance and music. The splendid fireworks on Bhagirathi embankment make the venue a picturesque vista that impresses the visitors no end. The festival is enjoyed by people of different age-groups, religions and cultural backgrounds. It not only tells the tale of the city's age-old splendour, but also marks the unity of its people and their love towards their cultural and traditional inheritance. Thousands of tourists from the other districts and states come for enjoying the famous festival every year.

Hazarduari Mela

HazarduariMela is also an attractive festival and which is conducted by the West Bengal State Tourism Department alongwith the Murshidabad District administration. HazarduariMela is held on an open sky stage keeping the Hazarduari palace in the backdrop. Between the palace and the Imambara on southern flank of the palace ground, the stalls are set up with various handicrafts of Murshidabad district like Belmetal, Sola crafts, Silk sarees,and handicrafts from ivory and wood products etc. The Mela also includes songs by local artists of Bauls and Fakirs of Murshidi and Marfati genre.

Commuting within Murshidabad

Intra City commuting is pretty efficient as it is majorly state run. Cars for hire, buses andcabs are easy to find. Many hotels also offer their private tour guides and cars by taking extra charges. Local taxi or buses are also easily available and they are cheap and readily available.

Tourism Characteristics of Murshidabad

- Basic feature of tourism of the Murshidabad is historical tourism.
- This district is also enriched with heritage tourism products.
- Tourist areas are not well developed but developing.
- Basic characters of rural tourismalso exist with rich historical tourism.
- Host communities are not well educated and trained in tourism perspective.
- Star rated hotels and excellent eating facilities are not available in this area.
- People are very innocent and helpful to the tourist.
- Government is taking interest for the development of the tourist areas from past few years.

Tourism attractions in Murshidabad District:

There are many tourism attractions in Murshidabad district. Some major attractions are described below:

1. The Hazarduari Palace is the main tourist attraction of Murshidabad district. Hazarduari means building of 1000 doors which was built in 1837 by Duncan McLeod for the Nawab Najim Humaun Jah, a descendant of Mir Zafar. This place building is one of the most important and significant tourist attractions of Murshidabad district and which is sprawling palace has been built on 41 acres of land. It has 900 hundred real doors and about 100 were later built ornamentally, 114 rooms and 8 galleries. It is now converted into an important museum and boasts a collection of nearly 3,000 artefacts. with an exquisite collection of unique paintings, armour, exhaustive portraits of the Nawabs, war-weapons of the Nawab and the British, swords used by Shiraj-ud-Daulla and his grandfather, Nawab Alibardi Khan and some vintage cars used by various Nawabs and their familiesworks of art that include

beautiful works of ivory from China and many other valuables items. The Palace was used for holding the "Durbar" and or various important meetings and other official works of the Nawabs. It was also used as the residence of the high-ranking British officials.

2. Nizamat Imambara is another important tourist attraction (spot) of this district which is standing parallel to the north side of the Palace Hazarduari and it was built in 1847 AD by Nawab NazimMansoor Ali Khan Feradun Jah, son of Humayun Jah it is no doubt the largest Imambara in Bengal.

3. Katra Mosque is situated on the Lalgola - Berhampur road, which was built by Murad Farash Khan, who is a devoted follower of Murshid Quli Khan (in 1723-24 AD). It is another striking tourist spot of Murshidabad and one of the most well maintained. It is a gorgeous building with having its huge domes and high minarets. A simple cemetery of the Nawab can be found below the front staircase. The mosque is also a tomb of MurshidQuli Khan who is buried under the flight of stairs comprising the entrance to the mosque from the eastern end.

4. Wasif Manzil (Palace) was built by Nawab Wasif Ali Mirza Khan. It is Located at the south end of the Hazarduari Palace.The palace is small but no doubt very beautiful and attractive for the tourists. The palace used to have an artificial hill and landscape on its side which got destroyed along with most of the palace in the earthquakes of 1867. The architecture of the place is very attractive. This palace is by the bank of the Ganga River.

5. Madina is a small mosque (Masjid) between the Palace and the Imambara. It is one of the most sacred Muslim places in West Bengal. It was made to replicate the tomb of Hazrat Muhammad's at Madina. Attractive matter is that, the original mosque's foundation had soil from Mecca, before it got destroyed in the fire. After that it was constructed with pious soil from Karbala. And it is the only surviving structuremade by Nawab Siraj-ud-

Doula.There are two minarets at the two ends of the mosque and measuring about 70 feet high and still exist. The architectural layout (plan) of this building is a rectangular and which has been divided into five inlets, each with having a curved entrance and the central one is the most noticeable one.There was a very good architectural arrangement for 700 Quran readers. The mosque has five domes and each of them used by a solo Namaz reader.

6. Jahan Kosha Cannon is a kilometre from Katra in the district Murshidabad. The 7 ton Cannon literally means the word 'Jahan Kosha' is 'the destroyer of the world'.JanardanKarmakar,a small craftsman at the time of Dhaka presently in Bangladesh, built the imposing cannon.It is 18 feet tall cannon.

7. Jafarganj Cemetery is located about a mile from the Hazarduari Palace. It is also called the Jafarganj Complex. Mir Jafar originally built this palace. But later the place was used for a cemetery for the family members of Mir Jafar like Mir Jafar's father Syud Ahmed Nazafi, Alivardi Khan's sister, Shahkhanum, Mir Jafar's widows, Munni Begam and Babbu Begam. These are the some of the important family members of Mir Jafar buried in this area.

8. KhoshBagh is a beautiful garden area of about eight acres of land. Thisgarden area actually used as a cemetery. It has the grave of NawabAlivardi Khan along with hismother, Siraj-ud-Doula and his wife Lutfannesha and some other members of the Nawab family.

9. Nasirpur Palace is built by the descendants of Debi Singh who was a tax collector of Murshidabad area in the early days of East India Company. ThisNasirpur Palace is certainly another major tourist attraction of Murshidabad district.

10. MotiJheel is a palace and a beautiful lake and which is about one km South of Lalbagh. This lake is still surviving but the palace perished. This is one of the few

places that reflect the characters of both the Indian and the British history.This beautiful horse-shoe shaped lake was excavated by Nawazesh Mohammad. He was husband of the famous Ghasseti Begum. Later this palacewas used as the residence for Lord Clive, Warren Hastings and a host of other important British Lords. This palace was the home of Warren Hastings when he became the Political President at the Durbar of the Nawab Nazim (1771 - 73 AD). After that, Sir John Shoore, afterwards Lord Teinnmouth, also lived in this palace. Due to its affinity to the British officials, it got popularity as 'Company Bag' (nick name). To the east of Nawajesh Muhammad's mosque, is a small enclosure within which are four tombs and to the east of which and outside it is one tomb. And here lie the mortal remains of Shahamat Jang (alias Nawajesh Muhammad), Siraj-ud-Doula's younger brother, Ekram-ud-Doula and his Tutor, (Shumsheree Ali Khan) the General of Nawajesh Muhammad and Nurse of Ekram-ud-Doula.

11. Kathgola is located a few kilometres away from Hazarduari Place.This palace complex is built originally to entertain and hospitality purposes ofthe European and Muslim guests during their trade visits.The pace Kathgola (wood war house) acquires its name from the lumber yard that used to be functional in the area before the palace was built. Built ahead of its times, the place is more than just a palace.

12. Footi Mosque was established by Nawab Sarfaraz Khan and which is located at Kumrapore area that is towards the East of the Hazarduari Palace. The mosque is believed to be the brainchild of Sarfaraz Khan. The mosque could not be completed and is often rumoured among the people to have been built in one night.

13. The Bachchawali Tope (canon) was made between the 12th and the 14th century. Just Beside the old Madina this canon is kept for the tourists. It is popularly known as "Bacchewali Tope". This canon was test-fired only once after making. The result was not good one and it is stated

that as it let to the miscarriage of several pregnant women within 10 km. of the vicinity and it requires about 18 Kg of gun powder for a single shelling.

14. Barrack Square is another tourist spot in Murdhidabad district. There is a Saheed-bediat the south-western side of this Barrack Square. The oldest church of Murshidabad named Armenian Church which was built in 1858 A.D. There is a Dutch Cemetery also which was built in 1632 A.D. and which is taken over by the archaeological department, Govt. of India for heritage preservation.

15. Kherur Mosque is 2 km. away from Bhumisar. It is enriched with beautiful art works of terracotta. It is now taken over by the Archaeological Department, Government of India.

16. Residence of Zamindar of Nimtita is 5 km away from Bajitpur. Here Satyajit Roy has made shooting for his famous films 'Debi' and 'Jalshaghar'.In 1897 A.DManindra Narayan made Nimtita Hindu Theatre and where famous actor Sisir Bhaduri acted.

Accessibility:

The nearest airport is Netaji Subhas Chandra Bose International Airport in Kolkata. Murshidabad is around 182 km. distance from Kolkataairport. There are some well-connected rail way stations in this district. Though, Berhampur Court and Lalbagh Court Road railway stations are the best options for the tourist, those are coming from Kolkata side. It takes maximum5-6 hours from Kolkata to Berhampur and adjacent tourist areas via rail route.Berhampur and Kolkata are very well-connected to the rest of India via the road network. Buses play frequently from Kolkata, Siliguri, Burdwan, Durgapur etc. to various parts of Murshidabad.

Socio-Economic Impact of tourism in Murshidabad

The positive impacts of tourism on economical and

socio-cultural perspective are mentioned below-

- It creates employment opportunity for the local people concerned with tourism.
- It increases demand for local goods and services.
- Rural artisans get direct contact with the customers.
- Local small business is getting benefits.
- Development of market of the agro products and handicrafts.
- Rise income level.
- Reduce migration of rural people to urban areas.
- It generates foreign exchange which is positive for the state as well as the country, India.
- It generates government revenue from the tourists and tourism business concerned.
- Rural people are learning to use modern tools and technology from the tourists.
- Modernisation of agriculture and other rural activities.
- Provide higher standard of living.
- Improve culture, health and education of the rural communities.
- Cultural exchange and understanding through fairs and festivals.

Challenges and Opportunities of tourism in Murshidabad

Followings are some major challenges of tourism in Murshidabad district-

- The physical communication is big problem in the Murshidabad district for tourism development. Communication facilities are needed by developing roads, hotels and restaurants for foods and lodging hotels, drinking water, electricity, telephone, safety and security of the tourists and local communities etc.

- Financial support from the government or non-government organisations is not sufficient for proper maintenance and development of the tourism products.
- Most of the residents do not understand and speak English and Hindi. Language and education is the basic obstacle in communication between tourists and local people.
- Lack of basic education is a major problem in tourism in Murshidabad district.
- The guide plays a very important role in attracting tourists but trained tourist guide is not available in this district.
- Tax rate and execution policy is a problem in this field from both side's tourists and people with tourism business.
- Lack of clear government legislation for the tourist and residents.
- Lack of commitment by the public sector for the local business as well as tourists.
- Lack of linkages between micro, small and medium enterprises.
- Lack of business opportunity awareness and financial institutional support.
- Corruption and mismanagement of some local people and administration is also a problem.

Followings are some major opportunities of tourism in Murshidabad district

- Now the West Bengal government is giving priority focus on tourism sector especially on heritage tourism.
- The West Bengal government is currently has taken a comprehensive tourism policy. The state has begun its Beautiful Bengalcampaign to sensitize national

and international tourists about the many attractions of the state.

- Awareness among the residents are generating day by day for betterment of life.
- Local people are very innocent and having good mentality to provide best services to the tourists.
- Residents of the tourist sites are very helpful and having no mentality to cheat with the tourists.
- It canensure that it becomes a resource for development in remote and economically back worded regionslike a district Murshidabad in West Bengal.
- Tourism development at heritage sites in this district can bring improved income and living standard for the local communities concerned with tourism business.
- Maintenance and preservation of heritage sites and cultures of Murshidabad can help by creating awareness of the history, pride and civilization of the people of the district.
- Heritage products of Murshidabad are the source and symbol of identity of the district.
- The tourism sites of Murshidabad can play an important rolefor socio-economic development of the local people.
- There are huge opportunities for national and global recognition and identity in the world heritage list especially for the Hazarduari Place and Imambara.

Recommendation for tourism in Murshidabad District

There are the following recommendations are proposed which will enable the district (Murshidabad) to achieve the satisfied growth and development in infrastructures and in the tourist numbers.

- Right initiative should be taken. It is the main step

towards introducing the right initiatives to maximize tourist inflow.

- Regional connectivity should be improved through creation of roads, high speed passenger trains from Kolkata.
- High speed waterway connectivity may be introduced from Kolkata to Lalbag, Baharampore etc. on the Ganga River for improving connectivity.
- Accommodation facilities should be developed in selected unexplored destinations, the service levels should be upgraded by setting up new hotels, lodges, restaurants, recreational centres etc.in thoseareas.
- The West Bengal government should collaborate with other governments for promotion of various tourism circuits like Murshidabad as these states can combine their efforts and offer for comprehensive services and solutions.
- Loans and others financial support like subsidy, tax concession etc. should be given to the local communities for entrepreneurship development and development of the existing business on tourism.
- The government should emphasis on Public Private Partnership (PPP) model for infrastructural development and proper promotion of the tourist areas of the Murshidabad.
- The state government should increase the budget as the proper promotion of tourism in Murshidabad can be possible.
- Tourism infrastructure should be better in these fields like road, sanitation, water supply, hygiene, electrification, bank and ATM, social-security etc.
- Government should make some modern service infrastructures like guest house, rest house, hotel, local health centres etc. at the tourist places in this district.

- Government should arrange training program for the technical and non-technical persons associated with tourism services in Murshidabad district.
- Government should provide financial help for entrepreneurship development to the local community by providing attractive scheme.
- Murshidabad and adjacent districts may take into consideration to the tour operators for making logical tourism circuits based on the budget and time.
- The optimum utilization of internet may come of a lot of use as creation of innovative websites which can provide the opportunity to the local communities in district level to market their products directly online to potential customers.
- The state government and tour operators should make innovative marketing strategies by with the help of internet.

REFERENCES

1. Tull Walsh, J.H. A History of Murshidabad District (Bengal) with Biographies of some of its noted families. Jarrold and Sons.
2. Majumdar, P.C. (1905). The Musnud of Murshidabad (1704 -1904).
3. O'Malley, L. S. S. (1915). Bengal District Gazeetters (Murshidabad). Published by The Bengal Secretariat Book Depot, Calcutta.
4. Das, N. (2014). Murshidabad: Forgotten Capital of Bengal, Publisher: Marg Foundation.
5. Mamun, A.A. &Mitra, S. (2012). The Last King in India by Wajid Ali Shah (1822-87) "A Methodology for Assessing Tourism Potential: Case Study Murshidabad District, West Bengal, India", International Journal of Scientific and Research Publications. 2(9). ISSN 2250-3153
6. Mondal, D. (2012). Assessment of Tourism Carrying capacity for Hazarduari Palace Museum in Murshidabad Municipal town, West Bengal.ZENITH, International Journal of MultidisciplinaryResearch.2(8). ISSN 2231 5780

7. Anam, M.K. Indian Freedom Movement and Murshidabad District 1905-1947
8. Mukhopadhyay, S.C. British Residents at the Darbar of Bengal Nawabs Murshidabad 1857-72
9. Murshidabad affairs, 1821-1850: Records of Berhampur Collectorate, West Bengal
10. Das, A.Renaissance Revisited: Murshidabad (1853-1953)
11. Ministry of Tourism, Government of India. Report on the Working Group of Tourism, 12th Five-Year Plan (2012-17),
12. Report on India Tourism Statistics (2010).Ministry of Tourism, Government of India, Market Research Division.
13. Iatu, C. & Bulai, M (2011). New Approach in Evaluating Tourism Attractiveness in the Region of Moldavia (Romania).International Journal of Energy and Environment. 5(2): 165-174.
14. Constantin, M. ; Daniela-Luminia, C. & Mihaela, G. (2009). Tourism Potential and the Diminishing of Regional Disparities in Romania. pp-151-155 [web: http://steconomice.uoradea.ro/anale/volume/2009/v2-economy-and-business-administration/25.pdf]
15. Vander Merwe, J.H.; Ferreira, S.L.A. &Van Niekerk, A. (2008). A Spatial Gap-Analysis Of Tourism Development Opportunity In The Western Cape Province. Centre for Geographical Analysis, Stellenbosch University.
16. Morimoto, S. A Stated Preference Study to Evaluate the Potential for Tourism in LuangPrabang, Laos. [web: http://www.pigliaru.it/chia/Morimoto.pdf]
17. Bureau of Applied Economics and Statistics (Series-2001). District Statistical Handbook Govt. of west Bengal, Murshidabad.
18. Tcholeev, I. &Vodenska, M. Spatial Analysis of The Tourism Potential in Bourgas District. [web:http://www.datamap-bg.com/conference_cd/pdf/P1_316_Tcholeev_Vodenska.pdf]
19. Web: http://en.wikipedia.org/wiki/Murshidabad_district.
20. Web: http://murshidabad.nic.in/museum.htm.
21. Web: http://murshidabad.net/history/places-topic-hazarduari-Palace.htm.

10

Search Engine Optimization Enhance Brand Equity: A Marketing Mix Dynamic in Asian Markets

Dola Sarkar & Dr. Jadab Kr. Das

ABSTRACT

Presently global effect in the market place is one of the most important challenges faced by the companies in emerging markets. It is a difficult task for the managers to understand the changing preference of the customers and ability of the retail sectors to transform consumer demand in to purchase. Rapid growth of innovation, easy availability of different competitive products at cheaper rates, changing dynamics of the marketing tools, customers changing purchasing pattern and ways of engaging with shoppers, growth of disposable income, development of technology and growth in digital as well as social media are the big boost for changing marketing strategy in Asian markets (e.g., India and China). Despite resource constraints, marketer in emerging markets not only concentrate on brand performance related attributes, brand managers also need to focus upon the product related imagery attributes. As emerging economics have been occupied a good percentage of ROI in world market and growth is remarkable in recent years. So, in this context, it is critical to look at how SEO as a marketing-mix dynamic can be incorporated in formulating proper business strategies which can be a good blend of socio marketing challenge to achieve the success of an organization.

Key Words: Search engine optimization, visual effect, brand building, marketing mix dynamics

Introduction

The present concept of brand building is not only for brand response but to create a strongand positive loyalty relationship between customers and the brand. Search engine optimization (SEO) is the procedure of making an attractive design, coding or writing a website to develop the quality and visibility of the website of the company for the people using search engine, basically in the un-paid form. Theprovide opportunities to the marketers with SEO strategists by creating proactive campaigns to enhance company website that push satisfaction and immediate reactions to consumers while searching. Companies generally work hard to achieve higher ranking for their websites as because more frequently the sites appears at the top of the page and the possibility of visitto the site will be more for the user(Enge, et al,2012).To compete with other avenues and achieve higher ranking, SEO helps to provide diverse techniques, like increasing links from other websites to company web pages, reorganizing of the content of the website, editing the design, and develop new structure as well as coding changes (Shih, etal.2013). A successful SEO campaign is focused not only search engine ranking, but also put the company to stand with the best in competitive market to become the largest player in the industry. Jansen and Spink, 2006 identified that 73 percent of search engine users never look back beyond the first page of returned results. All SEO engaged brand recognized that there was average traffic rise by 19.8 percent in each year in 2014. (Nielsen-Ratings, 2015), although it was 18.1 percent in 2013 and after that 3 percent increase like 21 percent of total average site traffic in 2014.Presently there are millions of search engine in use in the market which include **Google, Yahoo, Epic, Khoj, MSN, ASK** etc. Data obtained from Net market share, 2013identified that Google obtained 83 percent score in the total market and most popular widely used sites(2013).So, it is really hard for a marketer to advertise or sell products after choosing the sites on a large scale. Advertisers today believe on web-user behaviour to know their immediate reaction and the message they carry from the visitor 'send. Based up on these, advertisers want to place advertise to catch the potential customers. The particular content or concept created by marketers on their brands to create awareness and these SEO initiative helps to grab the opportunities as well as generate customer reaction. Since the ratio of internet users has increased radically over a period of time, the application of SEO is increasing day by day and its relevancy has become more popular and useful for marketers and brand managers. This development shows the increasing demand of the online advertising and interactive technology, named as socialnetworking.Abraham in 2008 also proved evidence based up on different studies that online advertisement has a great influence on online and offline sales. A survey was conducted in 2010 on online advertising, where 1500 advertisers and agencies were studied and it was revealed the fact that more or less 90% of them engaged in SEO compared to 81% who acquired supported links (SEMPO, 2010).So all these studies added the importance and direct impact of online advertisement on sales. Again, Sands et al, 2010 conducted his study on 1,275 consumers, where he confirmed that sales revenue increased when consumers used the Internet to search for product information rather than in store purchases. Finally, it is observed and research confirms that online advertising has a positive impact on both online and offline sales (Rainer and Carsten, 2014).In this paper, we find the importance of SEO as a third media in the marketing mix tools, and how SEO can act as a positive communication tools to promote the brand in a more consistent way, helping to increase the brand value and customer easily recall the product feature during their purchase.

Research Objectives

This paperattempts to analyzeand extend its view on limited literature and previous empirical studies of the impact of SEO dimension on online advertisement and how marketer grab the opportunity to increase their market share in emerging markets.

- To analyze how emerging market economics present their product information in a unique way where the concepts can be extremely favorable to improve organic visibility.
- To know how Search Engine Optimization attract new potential customers and improve brand equity in emerging markets.
- To study how emerging market can improve online reputation and trade influence on other competitive products in the market.
- To know how SEO capitalize diverse meaningful keywords for customer acquisition and to acquire new meaningful back links to increase social connection.

In precise way, this work explores the nature and functional dynamism of this concept as well as diverse factors that influence online advertisement. The subject of the study is reflected as a new field in emerging economics, where the concept of search engine optimization looked newly in emerging markets and is still in early stages.

Search Engine works as a weapon of IMC (Integrated Marketing Communication) in emerging markets.

- To establish a comprehensive plan in emerging market that evaluates strategic roles in communication discipline, we should consider the efficiency of SEO techniques and how search engines work as well as what people are looking for. Integrated marketing communication tools are the primary advantage of the organization to create a brand identity as well as obtain a good traffic. To aware the customers about the product or service through different marketing channels of communication like advertisements, sales promotion, personal selling, social networking sites, internet selling are generally used by brand managers for making their brand successful and also a great return on investment as well as enhance the awareness of vendors.

Like other IMC tools we can summarize the major benefits and advantages of SEO in emerging markets:

- The prime benefit of SEO is that to put the company in top 10 ranking without any hassle, as it is easy for emerging consumers to avail the company address easily appearing on the first page of results.
- Easy to earn a good sharein the long run and consistent marketing strategy by SEO also can generate a steady traffic to the website and enrich consciousness of brands and vendors.
- Proper designing of site can easily optimize the benefit of SEO, which is much more cost effective than compared with other IMC tools. SEA (search engine advertisement) also can save much time and money to create value for brand recall and recognition.
- Increase sales of company's products and services are the results of increase online brand visibility of the particular company sites.
- SEO leads to make a crucial link between firms that use the Internet with their target customer.
- A good website design is the key to obtain a good volume of customer in emerging markets, which

has to be useful, easily accessible, reliable and giving proper value to the customer.

- If the company in emerging economics become aware the benefit of SEO, which will improve company image as well as market share, and also referral business online.

Through the steady promotional activity done by the organizations, the brand recognition and brand recall value will increase and also helpful for the customers to recollect the brand or particular feature of the product during their purchase. Consequently, helps to gain a profitable market share as well as brand equity.

Literature Review

Research on search engine optimization in emerging markets is considered very few. Most of the study was related with worldwide research on search engine in general (Ramaraj, 2013), search engine optimization in education (Gandour&Regolini, 2011), search engine advertisement (Jafarzadeh, 2011). Considering the previous studies, we will highlight the effectiveness of SEO and online advertisement in emerging markets to achieve a good traffic and optimize market share.SEO is aconcept of dynamic nature, which is defined by different authors in different ways. Seoguru technologies team (1998) proposed the numerous benefits that a company acquires by the use of search engine optimization technique. To create brand identity and cost-effective communication Search engine optimization is the most efficient tool. It assists the organization to increase their sales profit and ranks themselves at the top as the main players than with the other competitors in the market. A company can only have influence the rank of other competitors by the use of SEOs tool. Graham Charlton (2002) focused numerous benefits that a company can obtain by using SEOs, mainly for promotional purposes and brand value incensement. To achieve greater organizational visibility and market share and to get a long-term effect on the minds of the customers Search Engine Optimization is one of the very useful marketing tools. His paper basically identified diverse benefits which an organization can attain by spending a small amount of money as compared to their profits. The research of Vertexera in 2003 observed that how SEO works as a tool for establishing a brand. He also focused that the implementation of SEO will increase a site's visibility by selecting keywords, helping to produce good traffic, search engine policies and guidelines. Inadditions comprises dealing with design and content problems. With the radical change and progress of the technologies, the companies have indulged themselves in various alternatives for the successful promotion of their products and services and one of them is Search Enginewhich works as a useful marketing tool to promote the website of a companyand it is also very cost-effective marketing tool. Search Engine optimization is a proper structuring method and process of identification of different factors in a webpage which help to find easy accessibility when searchingfor a relevant query in the web page of a company and makes a fine blend of the different elements in the web site, so that it can carry the highest possible organic visibility (Zgang and Dimitroff, 2005).Cheffey, et al. (2006) observed thatSEO ismainly for proper positioning of company or its products and also it is a most structured approach.FurtherWenyu Dou in 2006 stated the importance of search engine optimization for positioning of parti :ular brand in the competitive environment. Comprehensive theories from different research fields have established the fact that SEO acts as a meaningful vehicle to create brand positioning in the e-commerce world. This device can optimally be used when 'search engine ranking schema' trigger the Internet users through brand feature priming mechanism. It is mostly noticeable when less regular and sophisticated user involves searching this internet site to fulfill their diverse queries. To build successful brand Search Engine Optimization is the best exercise for the organization which give best promotional results in a mostcost-effectivemanner (Word Stream Inc. 2009). To establish the brand in the market as well as to acquire new customer base Search marketing is most powerful and cost-effective tools. It generates the alertness of the brand in the competitive market to influence people and help to convince them to buy the product or encourage them for trial purchase. He also added that SEO is an ongoing process, not a one –time activity. Like others promotional tools that is personal selling, internet selling, social networking sites, search engine optimization is also another integrated marketing tools. Search engine optimization aids the organization in building a successful brand image. Aric, Michael V. University of Baltimore (2010) revealed the importance of communication to create awareness among the consumers and at the same time it is also helpful for rightly positioning of the brand in the minds of the customer. He also considered the significance of the use of various communication tools called integrated communication tools for successful communication system and for building a successful brand. At the same period Edward Charles (2010) talked over the mythologies about the optimization of the content. The mythology was based up on that how people consider their content would be changed and how actually they are through. So, the clear understanding about the process of optimization should be provided to the companies so that no further controversy should arise in future regarding the rank of the particular web page. As because the optimizers never deliver any assurances regarding the rank on the search engine,Search engine optimization (SEO) is a structured and systematic approach to gain the number of visitors to the site and also improving the membership in the particular company website, but not the quality of the search engine(Google, Search Engine Optimization Starter Guide, 2010).So ultimately the role of Search Engine Optimization is to achieve highest ranks or position and different sites like Google, Yahoo and MSN trying to be better ranked by one or several targeted search engines (Gandourand Regolini, 2011). For the improvement and ranking of a website of a company in search engine listings, SEO is the best set of technique in the market to get more likings, where the end user will choose to visit the site (Vryniotis, 2015).

Research Analysis and Discussion

Madlenak, et al, (2015) proposed in his research work that internet marketing tools increase thenumber of visitors through their business website. Comparing the effectiveness of search engine with other IMC tools, comparative analysis can be drawn to find the degree of dependence and competition between different categories of visitors in emerging markets both for personal and official use of website. A detail analysis of Asian markets and their usage rate of search engine tools generate good profit; we can segregate the emerging markets in to two major groups-

- China
- India

China

Dragon Social is one of the Chinese Social Media Marketing agencies in China, contributing Weibo and WeChat marketing services. With a varied international team, they are planning to expand global business at China. There are different powerful search engines in Chinese market which can be an encouraging prospect for the customer.Unlike most other countries, Google and Bing are generally rare used in China. Instead, there are few main companies which dominate in China market, they follow only one key engine, Baidu.According to Chinese Internet Network information centre has stated that there are in total 566 million people using in China and the number is gradually rising. After that in quarter 2017, Chinese search engine covered a total market of 18.76 billion Yuan. Although this is actually a decrease of revenue of 8.6% from the previous year in quarter one., it is the reason that users have begun to focus on single search engine rather than swapping between the biggest competitors.

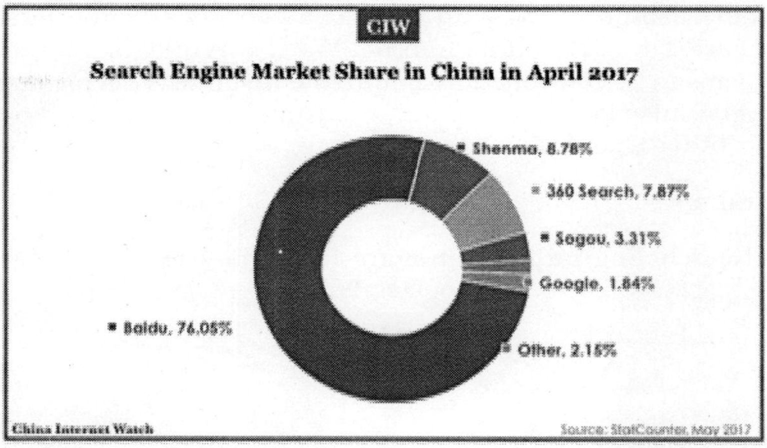

In the records of 2017,it looks like that Baidu has obtained around 80% market share in the year 2017(according to Chinainternetwatch.com), leading Chinese people to dub it "China's Google" After that Shenma hold 8.78%, 360 Search occupies 7.87%, Sogou cover 3.31% and Google is only 1.84%.There is, however, a range of different ways Chinese people can optimise SEO's using different Baidu products. Webmaster Tools allow customers to alter the scuttle rate through site, and answering questions about your company on Teiba, allows people to become more trusted. Baidu tends to put more importance on pages which are regularly updated and finally this makes it hard for new companies to break in to top pages gradually. Baidu also make a fine tune of their website in to a mobile friendly format which supports the people to serves to their own. They also run a chain of their websites like Wenku,Zhidao,Baike, Wei ZexiScandal, which tend to become on the first page. Mobile search engine facility seem to have more opportunity for taking the market away from Baidu.So, mobile search engine market at China would follow computer search engines, which seems that Chinese market is very competitive.The main top three search engines used are Baidu with 78.2%, Sogou at 7.9% and Easou at 4.9%, with other competitors at 9.0% (First quarter of 2017, China Internet Watch). While the market seems to be controlled by Baidu, the revenue is decreasing as because lack of trust and so customers may be turning to other search engines.

India

Search Engine market share in India from Jan 2016 to Dec 2016

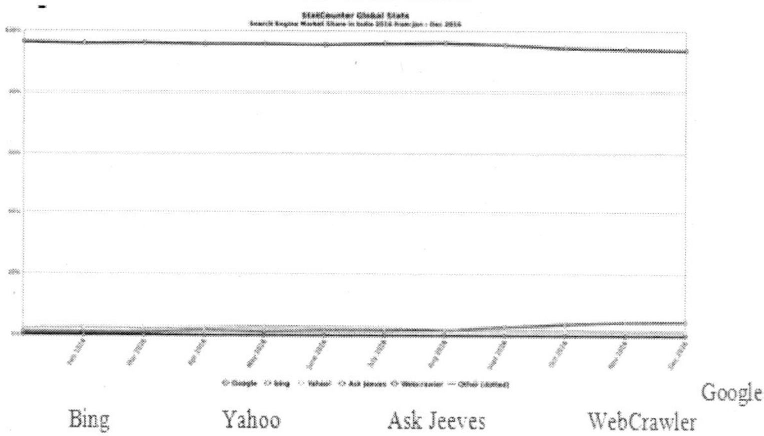

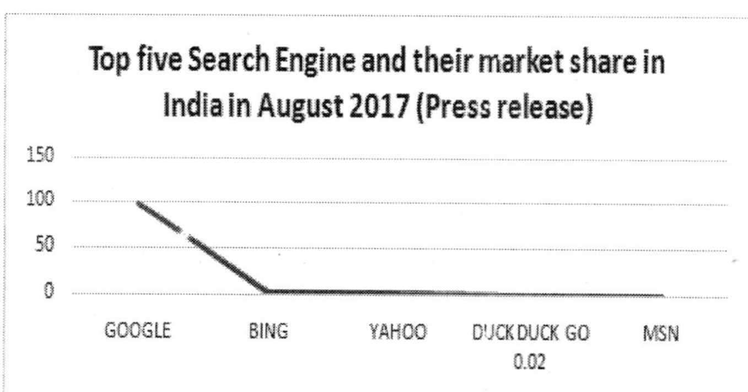

The above chart shows the different Search Engine and their market Share in India in August 2017.Here Google shows the leading position occupying almost 96.64%, Bing holds 2.14%, yahoo makes the market share 0f 1.16%, 0.02% for Duck Duck Go and finally MSN is for 0.01

Worldwide market share of leading search engine—A spread chart Analysis (From 2010 to 2015)

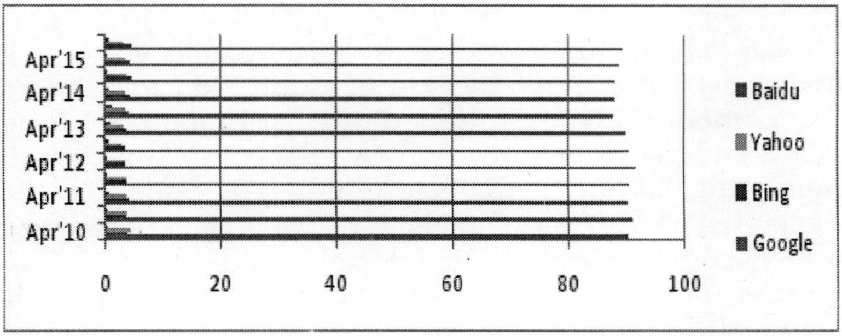

The Graph shows that starting fromthe year 2010 to 2015 the Google is in the lead position, followed by Bing, Yahoo and Baidu. Even the results are same for the next two consecutive years of 2016 (96%) and 2017(96.64%).Google even if under ever increasingload, is and remains the number one search engine and by using this search engine sites for the promotional purpose or advertisement of the product Indian companies aregenerating a buzz about the brand as well as about the product among the audience of the different target markets and making brand identity.Although Google governs mainly search and advertising markets worldwide, but its Android mobile operating system presently occupies 80% of the mobile device market. So,Google's major opening for the future is a handful of countries and as US and Europe has a huge mature mobile market, Google realizes a vast opportunity in emerging market also. In the next two years, Google presumes 1.2 billion smart phones business in an emerging country like Brazil, China, India, Indonesia, Mexico and Russia. The main barrier to reveal the potential market is giving a high performing, affordable smart phones to the customers.India has now become a key market for maximum tech companies in recent years. According to a report co-authored by Google last year, the growth of internet economy mainly for Southeast Asia's country is expected to grow 6.5-fold to reach $ 197 billion by 2025.

Conclusion

The search engine optimization is basically a growing and dynamic activity in case of promotion and brand recognition. With the initiation of new digital marketing tactics and the development of new segment such as content marketing, social media marketing, etc. Sofinally, the dependency of social signals and content marketing on search engine operation led to even more attention in present integrated approach of brand identity. And this integration can reach much further and beyond tactics.Search is and remains an affair of promises and relevancy should be there with the way people search in mind. So, search is a part of multi-channel customer drive and Google play the active role to confirm it.SEO contributes to optimize the website of the company and to increase the opportunity to get the higher ranking of searching online advertisement by increasing number of customers in emerging markets. Search engines like Google, social networking sites and different online business where website supports to find information about product or services.Research results show that objectives of the study are relevant and the companies in emerging markets are getting more customers by using SEO for online advertisement than companies using other communication tools. The popularity of search engine optimization is not only cost effective and leads better conversion rate as well as good marketing results, but also it goes beyond search in the definite sense to support social interaction.Search engines have constant updated their algorithms on one hand and negated the old and Sammy SEO tactics on the other hand, so all search engine customer or community need to understand the impact of these changes and come up with new ways to outwit the latest changes.

REFERENCES

1. Cheffey, D., Ellis-Chadwick, F., Mayer, R., Johnston;"Internet marketing Strategy, Implementationand Practice", Prentice Hall, Essex, page 349
2. Edward Charles, (2010); "myths about working ofSEOs", 4ps
3. Enge, E., Spencer, S., Stricchiola, J. and Fishkin, R. (2012);"The Art of SEO: Mastering Search Engine Optimization", 2nd ed., O'Reilly Media, Sebastopol, CA.
4. Gandour, A. and Regolini, A. (2011);"Web site search engine optimization: a case study of Fragfornet", LibraryHi Tech News, 2011, pp. 6-13, page 7
5. Graham Charlton;"business benefits of SEOs". journal of advertising
6. Jafarzadeh H., Aybüke A. and D'Ambram J. (2011);"Factors Affecting the Success of Businesses in Effective Utilization of Search Engine Advertising: Research-in-Progress". SigIQ pre-ICIS workshop
7. Jansen, B.J. and Spink, A. (2006);"How are we searching the World Wide Web? A comparison of nine search enginetransaction logs", Journal of Information Processing and Management, No. 42, pp. 248-63.
8. Laric, Michael V. University of Baltimore (2010);" the role of IMC in Brand Building"
9. Madleòák, R., Madleòáková, L., □vadlenka, S, &Salava,D. (2015). "Analysis of Website Traffic Dependence on use of Selected Internet Marketing Tools",ProcediaEconomics and Finance, 23, pp. 123-128.
10. Nelsen-NetRatings (2015); "Nielsen Net Ratings Search Engine Ratings: Natural Search's Growth Explosion, andwhatitmeans for SEO "
11. RamarajPalanisamy (2013); "Evaluation of Search Engines: A Conceptual Model and Research Issues", International Journal of Business and Management; Vol. 8, No. 6.

12. Rainer Olbrich Carsten D. Schultz, (2014);"Multi-channel advertising: does print advertising affect search engine advertising?", European Journal of Marketing, Vol. 48Iss 9/ 10 pp. 1731 – 1756

13. SEMPO Annual State of Search Survey (2010).

14. SEO Guru Technologies Team, (1998); "Branding through SEOs".

15. Shih, B.Y., Chen, C.Y., & Chen, Z.S. (2013);"An EmpiricalStudy of an Internet Marketing Strategy for SearchEngine Optimization",Human Factorsand Ergonomics inManufacturing& Service Industries, 23(6), pp.528–540.

16. Vertexera(2003); "Benefits of Search Engine Optimization", Journal of marketing research.

17. Vryniotis, VasilisWebSEO analytics blog (2015); Is Google PageRank still important in Search Engine Optimization?

18. Wenyu Dou (2006); "brand positioning strategy using search engine marketing", business today marketingJournal

19. Word Stream Inc., (2009);"search engineoptimization, best practices", ANA Educator Procedures.

20. Zgang, J. and Dimitroff, A. (2005);"The impact of webpagecontent characteristics on webpage visibility in search engine results (Part II), Information Processing and Management" 41, pp. 691-715.

11

Finding Out the Correlation Between Reported Crime Against Children and Literacy Rate in India

Dr. Sourav Gangopadhyay & Dr. Jayeeta Majumder

ABSTRACT

This paper is concerned about the growing rate of crime against children. Crime against children is a curse of any nation; there are lots of causes behind those. Some researchers have pointed out that literacy is playing a vital role in it but others do not think so. Some of them have not be able to find any correlation with the literacy. In this paper we are trying to find out the relation between child abuse and literacy in Indian prospective. We have collected secondary data from different government website like handbook of statistics on Indian states Published by Reserve Bank of Indialiteracy Rate of 28 states of India in the year 2011, were collected. Whereas from the crime in India 2016 published by National Crime Records Bureau, the crime against children is collected. Regression analysis has done, and it is found that there is no correlation existing between literacy and the crime against children.

Keywords: Crime, children, literacy, Reserve Bank of India, National Crime Record Bureau.

Introduction

Crime against children is depending upon several factors among them illiteracy is important. (Gil, 1970). Researchers have found that behind every juvenile sexual harassment there is some issue on educational background of the culprit (Sarkar, 2002). Most of the juvenile injustice came from illiterate families. Less educated parents are not able to provide good parenting as study suggested but also it was seen that juvenile injustice is existing in families having high educational background (Bhattacharya, 2013). Another research paper showed that the crime is committed more in less educated family than high educated family (Hancen, 1992). It was also seen that uneducated parents are not serious enough about their children's development (Singha, 2017).

Research Methodology

We have done Cross sectional study by taking secondary data; data are collected from Different Website. From handbook of statistics on Indian states Published by Reserve Bank of Indialiteracy Rate of 28 states of India in the year 2011, were collected. Whereas from the crime in India 2016 published by National Crime Records Bureau, the crime against children is collected. The states which are included in the study are - Andhra Pradesh, Arunachal Pradesh, Assam, Bihar, Chhattisgarh, Goa, Gujarat, Haryana, Himachal Pradesh , Jammu and Kashmir, Jharkhand, Karnataka, Kerala, Madhya Pradesh, Maharashtra, Manipur, Meghalaya, Mizoram, Nagaland, Odisha, Punjab, Rajasthan, Sikkim, Tamil Nadu, Tripura, Uttar Pradesh, Uttarakhand and West Bengal, so total 28 states are taken in the study. Firstly literacy rate of 28 states of India and crime against children rate of 28 states are collected. Regression analysis has done with the help of SPSS 17th version.

Data Analysis

We have analyzed whether there is any correlation with the literacy and crime against children existing or not we used 17th version of Statistical Package for the Social Sciences or SPSS software. To see how literacy is putting impact on the crime against children we have done linear regression. The descriptive analysis shows the following result.

	Mean	Standard Deviation	N
Crime Rate Against Children	3273.37	4463.68	27
Literacy Rate	76.40	7.67344	27

The above chart is showing the descriptive study of the study. Total 27 states are included in the study the mean of crime rate against children is 3273.37 and the mean literacy rate is 76.40.

Correlation:

		Crime Rate Against Children	Literacy Rate
Pearson Correlation	Crime Rate Against Children	1.000	.235
	Literacy Rate	.235	1.000

The above table is showing the result of pearson correlation among correlation between crime rate against children and Literacy rate. According to the table correlation value is .235 existing between two variables. So it can be concluded that correlation between two variables is very weak.

Model Summary

Model	R	R square
1	.235	.055

The R square value is .055 so it means the model summary indicates an poor R-Square values it can be said that the regression model is not fitted to describe the dependent variable by the help of independent variables.

Model	Unstandardized Coefficients		Standardized Coefficients	t
	B	Std. Error	Beta	
Constant	-7161.747	8681.481		-.825
Literacy	136.591	113.088	.235	1.208

Y (Crime against Children) = -7161.747+136.591x literacy

Discussion:

The above analysis shows that there are no correlations with the literacy rate and the number of reported crime against children. In many research paper confirms that the crime against children is not depending upon literacy rate. Though some researchers have found significant relation is existed between two variables but most of them are not found any. Crime against children is a complex problem which is associated with multiple and complex causes. Literacy is playing some role in it but it is not regarded as the only causes. Without removing those causes crime against children cannot be controlled.

Conclusion

In our country children are victimized by many reasons which are enough to create scarred for their life which is bad for any nations. It is always immensely harmful for our society. In this regard our legal system is supposed to play a vital role in it. Rigid law, justice and some implementation of moral and social value could play a vital role in it. Both social support and community support are the main necessity to prevent it. We should also consider that the paper is only concentrated on the reported crime against children but there are many instance where committed crimes are not reported because of ignorance and many other factors. So we should think about it and we should provide enough opportunities to people to report the incidence also creating awareness on the nature and the way to report the crime to the concern authority is became necessary.

REFERENCES

1. Swain, J. (2002). Child Abuse in Orissa with Special Reference to Institutionalised Juvenile Delinquency.
2. Singha, R. (2017). Crime Intent Among School Adolescents Of Himachal Pradesh In Relation To Home Environment, School Environment, Media And Peer Influence.
3. Chandrashekar, S.V. (2014). Offences against Children: Criminal Justice and Social issues in India. International Research Journal of Social Sciences. 3(7). 10-12.
4. Bhattacharya, M. (2013). Expanding Horizons of the Law on Juvenile Delinquency and Its Practice.

12

Generation of Marketable Enzyme as Byproduct of Grape Pomace Bioconversion - Creation of Asset from Waste

Dr. Shamba Chatterjee

ABSTRACT

Microorganisms produce a vast array of enzymes which have been exploited commercially over a long period. Amongst them hydrolytic enzymes, especially pectinolytic enzymes, are a group of heterogeneous enzymes involved in hydrolyzing pectic substances and are widely distributed in higher plants and microorganisms. In a recent approach, grape pomace, the main waste in the wine industry, has been revealed to be the sole nutrient source for solid state fermentation to produce hydrolytic enzymes (cellulases, xylanases and pectinases) using fungal sources. This brief approach aims to provide a simple direction to the present scenario of hydrolytic enzyme production by nonconventional way using grape pomace as potential solid state fermentation substrate, which in turn will help us to fulfill the uprising market demand of those enzymes and environmental friendly waste management of grape pomace.

Keywords: Grape pomace, hydrolytic enzymes, solid state fermentation, Agro-Industrial Waste Management

Introduction

Grapes are one of the most vital fruit crop in the world and a major part of it has been utilized for making wines (about 68% of the world's total production) [1]. Wine manufacturing process yields a lignocellulosic waste, well versed as pomace. It is the residue left after juice production and derived from grape skins, seeds and pieces of stem. Low nutritional value and presence of anti-nutritional factors (phenolics) responsible for inhibition of microflora in rumen, made them unpopular as animal food. Beside several environmental problems, they potentially inhibit germination process which also limits their wide use as fertilizers [2, 3]. However, its agro-industrial implications can be regarded as of stout importance which in turn reduces pollution problems. In recent days, there has been a growing trend towards the utilisation of the solid-state fermentation (SSF) technique to produce higher enzyme titres over traditional submerged fermentation (SmF) process [4-7]. Grape pomace while being used as substrate in SSF, can generate a diverse array of products, namely ethanol [8] gluconic acid [9], carotenoids [10], xanthan [11] or citric acid [12]. Alternatively, it can also be exploited to yield a variety of enzymes, particularly from moulds [13, 14].

Agro-Industry Wastes

Around 1.3 billion tons of the total food produced globally for human consumption is wasted every year. In the European Union countries, food waste amounts to 89 million tons of food per year, while total agricultural residue production (crop residues that are not consumed as food) amounts to 367 million tons per year [15]. Most of the residue is consumed at the farm level as animal bedding and fodder and various horticultural implications. Various studies have been carried out over the past few decades exploring the successful utilization of agro-industry waste as a possible raw material for the production of value-added products. Most of these studies have been conducted in countries whose economies are profoundly dependent on agriculture. In this context, the wine industry produces millions of tons of residues widely known as grape pomace after fermentation, which portrays a waste management issue both ecologically and economically [16]. Researchers are continuously searching for suitable options to convert lignocellulosic residues of agro-waste as a raw material for the production of various enzymes (for example, a cellulases, xylanases and pectinases), that act on polysaccharides [17].

The Substrate

In countries like Spain, Italy and France, grape pomace, or marc, is one of the principal sources of lignocellulosic residue from the wine industry scoring about 250 million kilograms per annum (Fig. 1). Its chemical composition is rich in the main nutrients needed for the growth of a broad range of microorganisms. White grape pomace (Palomino fino variety) is of utmost importance amongst the available varieties and comprises a high carbohydrate content with the fibre representing about 50% of the total mass [18]. A detailed introspection reveals lignin as the foremost constituent of the fibre comprising 64% in the pips and 59% in the skin. Rest constituents of the fibre are hemicelluloses (18% of the fibre in pips and 31% in skin) and cellulose (17.75% and 6% in pips and skin). Pectin is present as a minor constituent reaching only a 0.25% of fibre in pips and 4% in skin. In general, freshly pressed white grape pomace are collected and preserved at – (20-24)°C. These when needed for experimental studies can be dried at 60°C for 48 h followed by commercial milling (mean diameter D50) and finally sieved before autoclaving at 121°C for 20 min [19]. Before one starts with the fermentation procedure a detailed chemical analysis of the contents are carried out by analyzing moisture and ash content, glucose, free amino nitrogen

Fig. 1: Different approaches of grape pomace utilization.

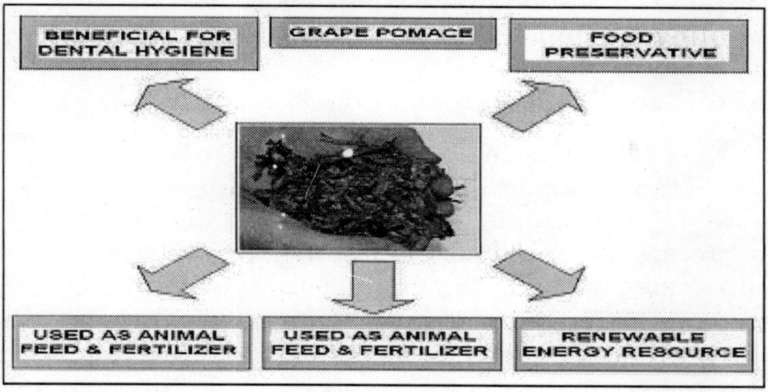

Fig. 2: Schematic presentation of Solid State Fermentation (SSF) Procedure.

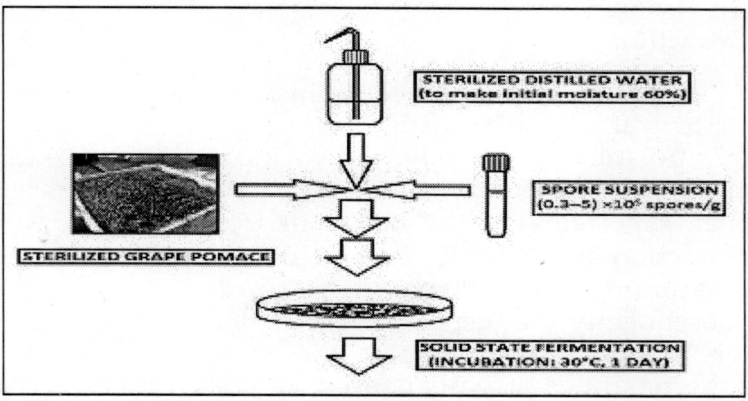

(colorimetric), total nitrogen (measured as Total Kjeldahl Nitrogen) and phosphorus (colorimetric).

Microorganisms Involved

An *Aspergillus awamori* strain (NRRL 3312 as well as 2B.361 U2/1) is generally propagated and preserved using 5% whole-wheat flour and 2% agar slants at 4°C. Next, either of them is resuspended with Tween 80 for the fermentation process. Finally, experimental set up needs a specific quantity of spore suspension around (0.3–5) x 10^5 spores/g of solid grape pomace counted in a Neubauer Counting Chamber [19, 20].

Solid State Fermentation (SSF) Procedure

The production of hydrolytic enzymes by A. awamori in SSF can be achieved by pouring required amount of spore suspension into petri dishes (9 cm in diameter) and the process can be initiated by adding 10 g of the autoclaved solid grape pomace. Next, the plates are generally incubated in triplicate under stable conditions at 30°C without stringent maintenance of pH. Analysis of the plates has usually been carried out at specific time intervals (Fig. 2). Attention must be taken or drawn while setting the initial moisture content (60% w/w) [19, 20].

Extraction

Post-fermentation procedure involves pooling the entire content of each petri dish (approximately 10 g) into 50 ml of distilled water followed by incubation for 30 min at 30°C and at 150-220 rpm in a rotary shaker. It has also been reported that the optimum temperature for the extraction lies within the range of 4–20°C, reaching maximum enzyme activities around 32 IU/gds. Subsequently, the suspension is centrifuged at 10000 rpm for 10 min at 4°C. Finally, the enzymatic extract in supernatant is usually stored at -20°C until further enzymatic analysis [19, 20]. Different criteria must be taken into considerations as follows: type of solvent, extraction temperature, time of extraction, stirring rate, volume of solvent and number of extraction steps (e.g. successive repetition of extractions).

Enzymatic Analysis Methods

A diverse range of experiments can be further implemented for enzymatic analysis. Initially, the reducing sugars produced are measured by a modified dinitrosalicylic acid method (DNS) which is expressed in terms of glucose concentration using a calibration curve [21, 22]. Cellulase activity is assayed using carboxymethyl cellulose (CMCase) by DNS method as mentioned in the above reference. Xylanase and exopolygalacturonase (exo-PG) activities are evaluated by determining reducing sugars released during hydrolysis of birchwood xylan and pectin, respectively [19]. On the other hand, endopolygalacturonase (endo-PG) activity can be estimated viscometrically by means of a Cannon-Fenske routine viscosimeter. Finally, the pH and moisture contents should also be taken into considerations [19].

Hydrolytic Enzymes as Product

Cellulase

Three key enzymes are involved in the depolymerisation of cellulose into component glucose molecules, viz., endoglucanase (E.C. 3.2.1.4), exoglucanase or cellobiohydrolase (E.C. 3.2.1.176) (E.C. 3.2.1.91) and â-glucosidase (E.C. 3.2.1.21). They belong to the glycoside hydrolase family and catalyze the cleavage of glycosidic bonds [23]. These enzymes are commercially important, following their key role in bioethanol production [24]. Additionally, cellulases have potential application in industries ranging bread, brewing, textiles, detergents, paper and pulp sectors [25].

Xylanase

Xylanases (E. C. 3.2.1.8, 1,4-â-xylanxylanohydrolase) break down xylan, an integral part of plant polysaccharide. Xylan is made of a xylose-residue backbone, with each subunit linked by a â-1,4-glycosidic bond and can be branched with D-glucuronic acid or D-arabinofuranoside [26]. This group of enzymes is produced by various bacterial and fungal species. Filamentous fungi synthesize xylanases and secrete it into the media in large quantities in comparison to bacteria [27]. This consortium of enzymes consists of endoxylanases, â-xylosidases, ferulic acid esterase, p-coumaric acid esterase, acetylxylan esterase and á-glucuronidase. Xylanases have broad applications in food, biomedical, animal feed and bioethanol industries [26, 28, 29]. Different conditions for the successful extraction of xylanase and exo-poligalacturonase have already been evaluated by solid state fermentation on grape pomace employing *Aspergillus awamori* [30].

Pectinase

Pectinases catalyzes the disintegration of pectin-containing compounds and can be classified into two groups according to their mode of action. Pectin esterases catalyze the de-esterification of methyl groups in pectin to yield pectic acid, whereas Depolymerase enzymes cleave the glycosidic bonds in pectic acid to release various simpler compounds. On the other hand, Protopectinases solubilize protopectin into highly polymerized forms of soluble pectin [31]. This group of enzymes is used in the fruit juice industry and wine making for clarification and removal of turbidity in the finished product [32]. Grape pomace has been extensively used in studies to determine their efficacy as suitable substrates for pectinase production [33].

Market Potential:

The global enzyme industry is flourishing with its increasing demand. It was worth almost $4.8 billion in 2013 and by 2018 became around $7.1 billion. Enzymes are vastly utilized for the production of different products that we employ in our everyday lives [34]. Moreover, recent interest in bioenergy has led to higher demand for enzymes applicable in the biofuel sector [35]. On the other hand, they can be produced for several industrial processes by using recombinant DNA technology and protein engineering. Therefore, decreasing the cost of enzymes can increase the market potential of its value-added products. Additionally, worldwide winemaking scenario has already unveiled the benefits achieved when a waste management policy is implemented [36].

Conclusion

Grape pomace has a vast potential as a budding substrate for the production of hydrolytic enzymes in commercial and research purposes. Chemical composition of pomace facilitates the growth of a wide range of microorganisms. On the other hand, its low cost has raised its acceptability. Several outcomes from researches have added the following inputs:

- Similar growth patterns and rise in activity of enzymes at initial stages have been observed which in turn is highly comparable with corresponding values in the literature.
- While moisture content and addition of extra carbon sources has resulted in utmost influence, particle size was of less influence on enzyme productivity.
- Solvent selection is another important criterion of concern (Tween 80 is a sound choice).
- Optimization of the temperature for enzyme extraction (especially for xylanase and exopolygalacturonase) has been found to be 4°C in order to assure thermal stability of enzymes.
- Time of extraction is not significant for the process outcome.
- Stirring rate is found to be a variable factor while 150 rpm is the maximum recommended for xylanase.
- Increase in the amount of solvent leads to an increase in the enzymatic activity extracted.
- Recent research has evidenced enhanced levels of activity of exo-PG, xylanase or CMC-ase obtained by using a mixture of grape pomace and orange peels (a natural source of pectin, cellulose and

hemicellulose) in solid state fermentation (SSF) or submerged fermentation (SmF).

Grape pomace in form of large volumes of solid wastes, residues and by-products are generated throughout the year as a consequence of agricultural and agro-food industries, produced either in the primary agroforestry sector or by secondary processing industries. Thereby, the bioprocessing of these residues can potentially help to solve environmental problems associated with their disposal. Consequently, a wide range of valuable and usable products can be recovered from what was earlier considered waste and help in suitable agro-waste management process.

REFERENCES

[1] Patil, V. K. et al., "Grape" In: Salunkhe DK, Kadam SS, editors, Handbook of fruit science and technology, New York: Marcel Dekker 1995, pp. 7–37.

[2] Sánchez, A., Ysunza, F., Beltrán-García, M.J., and Esqueda, M., J. Agric. Food Chem. 2002, 50, 2537–2542.

[3] Negro, C., Tommasi, L., and Miceli, A., Bioresource Technol. 2003, 87, 41–44.

[4] Viniegra-González, G., In E. Glindo, and O.T. Ramírez (Eds.), Advances in Biprocess Engineering II, Kluwer Academic Publishers, Dordrecht 1998. pp. 123–136.

[5] Viniegra-González, G., Favela-Torres, E., Aguilar, C. N., de Jesus Rómero-Gomez, S., Dýìaz-Godýìnez, G., and Augur, C., Biochem. Eng. J. 2003, 13, 157–167.

[6] Pandey, A., Biochem. Eng. J. 2003, 13, 81–84.

[7] Ramachandran, S., In: A. Pandey, C.R. Soccol, C. Larroche (Eds.), Current Developments in Solid-state Fermentation, Springer Science/Asiatech Publishers, Inc., New York, USA/ New Delhi, India. 2007, 230–252.

[8] Hang, Y. D., Lee, C. Y., and Woodams, E. E., Biotechnol. Lett. 1986, 8, 53–56.

[9] Buzzini, P., Gobbetti, M., Rossi, J., and Ribaldi M., Biotechnol. Lett. 1993, 15, 151–156.

[10] Buzzini, P., and Martini, A., Bioresource Technol. 2000, 71, 41–44.

[11] Stredonsky, M., and Conti, E., Process Biochem. 1999, 34, 581–587.

[12] Hang, Y. D., and Woodams, E. E., Biotechnol. Lett. 1985, 7, 253–254.

[13] Rodríguez Couto, S., Rodríguez, R., Gallego, P. P., and Sanromán, A., Acta Biotechnol. 2003, 23, 62–64.

[14] Viniegra-González, G., Biochem. Eng. J. 2003, 13, 157–167.

[15] Searle, S.M.C., ICCT: Washington, DC, USA, 2013.

[16] Fontana, A. R., Antoniolli, A., and Bottini, R., ýJ. Agric. Food Chem. 2013, 61(38), 8987–9003.

[17] Ravindran, R., and Jaiswal, A., Bioengineering. 2016, 3, 30.

[18] Igartuburu Chinchilla, J. M., Tesis Doctoral, Servicio de Publicaciones de la Universidad de Cádiz, Spain 1989.

[19] Botella, C., de Ory, I., Webb, C., Cantero, D., and Blandino, A., Biochem. Eng. J. 2005, 26, 100–106.

[20] Belén Díaz, A., de Ory, I., Caro, I., and Blandino, A., Food Bioprod. Process. 2012, 90, 72–78.

[21] Miller, G. L., Anal. Chem. 1959, 31, 426–428.

[22] Chatterjee, S., Biswas, S., Tripathy, A., and Sinha. S., Proceedings of "Prasanskaran-2012", 3rd Industry-Academia National Conference on "New Product Development: An Emerging Emphasis & Integral Part of Industrial Growth", Department of Food Technology, Haldia Institute of Technology, Haldia.

[23] Juturu, V., and Wu, J.C., Renew. Sustain. Energy Rev. 2014, 33, 188–203.

[24] Singhania, R.R., Saini, J.K., Saini, R., Adsul, M., Mathur, A., Gupta, R., and Tuli, D.K., Bioresour. Technol. 2014, 169, 490–495.

[25] Ferreira, N.L., Margeot, A., Blanquet, S., and Berrin, J.-G., Biotechnol. Biol. Trichoderma. 2014, 245–261.

[26] Harris, A.D., and Ramalingam, C., J. Exp. Sci. 2010, 1, 1–11.

[27] Knob, A., Beitel, S.M., Fortkamp, D., Terrasan, C.R.F., and Almeida, A.F. de, Biomed. Res. Int. 2013, 2013, 1–8.

[28] Das, S.P., Ravindran, R., Ahmed, S., Das, D., Goyal, D., Fontes, C.M.G.A., and Goyal, A., Appl. Biochem. Biotechnol. 2012, 167, 1475–1488.

[29] Goswami, G., and Pathak, R., Int. J. Basic Clin. Pharmacol. 2013, 2, 237.

[30] Díaz, A., Caro, I., de Ory, I., and Blandino, A., Enzyme Microb. Technol. 2007, 41, 302–306.

[31] Sakai, T., Sakamoto, T., Hallaert, J., and Vandamme, E.J., Adv. Appl. Microbiol. 1993, 39, 213–294.

[32] Servili, M., Begliomini, A.L., Montedoro, G., Petruccioli, M., and Federici, F., J. Sci. Food Agric. 1992, 58, 253–260.

[33] Botella, C., Diaz, A., de Ory, I., Webb, C., and Blandino, A., Process Biochem. 2007, 42, 98–101.

[34] Jegannathan, K.R., and Nielsen, P.H., J. Clean. Prod. 2013, 42, 228–240.

[35] Phitsuwan, P., Laohakunjit, N., Kerdchoechuen, O., Kyu, K.L., and Ratanakhanokchai, K., Folia Microbiol. 2013, 58, 163–176.

[36] Beres, C., Costa, G.N.S., Cabezudo, I., da Silva-James, N.K., Teles, A.S.C., Cruz, A.P.G., Mellinger-Silva, C., Tonon, R.V., Cabral, L.M.C., and Freitas, S.P., Waste Manage. 2017, 68, 581-594.

13

Simultaneous Management of Processing Industries, Environment and Sustainable Development

Dr. Niladri Chakraborty

ABSTRACT

From the law of conservation of energy (first law of thermodynamics), energy is conserved for both reversible and irreversible processes. But available energy or exergy is conserved only in reversible process and it destroyed either partially or completely in all irreversible process. Most of the natural phenomenon and engineering processes are irreversible process. So, exergy and entropy are decreasing and increasing respectively day by day. Therefore, shelf life of Earth and longevity and performance (efficiency) of machines / devices are decreasing as time progresses. Time always progresses into forward direction. In this sense engineers and managers have a big role to overcome it. It is now time to wake-up for them. The decreasing tendency of exergy and increasing tendency of irreversibility of processing industries have to solve for the making of pollution free environment and sustainable development. If not, the future generation survival will be doubtful and non-curable.

Keywords: Energy, Exergy, Process, Irreversibility, Environment, Sustainable development.

Introduction

From the 21-st century the industrial growth and development in our country are gradually increasing[1]. Out of these industrial areas Food Processing is the key industry where the development is remarkable. For sustainable development the energy utilization is the key to success. A less expensive and steady energy supply is requirement for socio-economic development. Never the less, for the long term sustainability of earth's ecosystems the management of three parameters viz. 'proper energy utilization', 'productivity' and 'safe/save environment' are the major requirement to reach the goal for benefits of society.

A newly term introduced in processing industries as an "*exergy*" which belongs to the quality of energy actually supplied for processing[2]. Hence, the *exergy* can surely controlling factor to impact on our environment. If the exergy efficiency is good (in the sense of increasing mode) then the loss of energy or energy emissions to the environment will be decreased.

Sustainable development encourages for increasing exergy and energy efficiency. Therefore, for the sustainability of energy to be used humans(particularly who deals on this area) must have concerned about not also loss of energy quantity, but they have also keeping in mind about loss of exergy. Since, exergy parameter helps to indicate the available energy and its usefulness (by the help of irreversibility calculation) for the processing. In a process, if exergy reaches to 100% then there is no impact leads to process operation into the environment. Similarly, if exergy is 0% then there will be highest impact on environment and hence sustainable development becomes to zero. So, we have to manage exergy anyway by good technical and ethical practices.

Technical Terms, Idea and Impact

Exergy is related with available energy and reversible

work performed in any thermodynamic process. Generally, maximum energy obtained by device (s) is called the available energy[3]. During process, the heat lost to the surroundings is termed as non-available energy. Therefore,

Total energy supplied to the processing = Available energy (Exergy) + Non-available energy (Lost or waste heat to the surroundings)

In any device such as heat-exchanger, available energy transfers from hot fluid to cold fluid and during transfer some available energy is lost. Hence, entropy of that process is increased and irreversibility is increased. So, some work is lost during process and actual work or useful work ultimately achieved. One can say,

Actual work or useful work = (Reversible work or maximum work) – (Lost work or Irreversibility).

So, from the above we concluded that if exergy is more then lost energy is less for a constant energy supplied for any processing. That means less energy lost not only to get more useful work but it enhances more productivity with less environment pollution and more sustainable development- which is a primary ambition of any good manufacturing practice (GMP) of any process unit. Hence, one can say that the good impact on environment to enhance economical and sustainable development is possible onlyif loss of heat and / or work is /are notable less.

Effectiveness

The efficiency of a system indicates the ratio of work available (exergy) to the heat supplied to the system but it is not a measure of fraction of maximum useful work actually utilized. The function of maximum available work (for reversible process) which is actually utilized is known as *effectiveness*[4]. It is defined as a ratio of increase in availability of the surroundings as the work is delivered by the system to the loss of availability of the system.

The effectiveness of heating (or expansion) process by a system is calculated by

€ = (Increase in exergy of the surrounding) / (Loss of exergy of the system).

The effectiveness of cooling (or compression) process by a system is calculated by

€ = (Increase in exergy of the system) / (Loss of exergy of the surrounding).

For reversible process, € = 1 and for irreversible process, € < 1.

Most of the processes are purely irreversible process i.e. € < 1, loss of exergy of the system or surroundings are greater than the gain of exergy either surroundings or system respectively. That means loss of exergy is not a beneficial effect for any process. But real thing is that as per physical concept of entropy available energy (exergy) of the universe decreases continuously due to all practical real processes and cycles. Therefore, it is concluded that for the increasing and decreasing of entropy and exergy respectively day by day it will not far away when universe will face a lot of challenges in future for its global warming, less efficient devices and less useful work from the processing unit. Careful and systematic technical managerial skill is necessary to solve these types of technical problems.

Role of Management

The term management roles refer to specific categories to managerial behavior[5].Mintzberg's ten managerial roles are described into three groups: Interpersonal relationships, Transfer of information and decision making at the right time.

Interpersonal role: It involves the people for their duties which are methodological and symbolic in nature. Transfer of information: Involves receiving, collecting and transferring the information. Decisional roles: This is the key success of any management skills (Right time and right decisions to take and implement)

Figure 1: Role of Engineering and Management on Maximum Exergy / Effectiveness of process and Utilization of maximum Energy to meet Sustainable development.

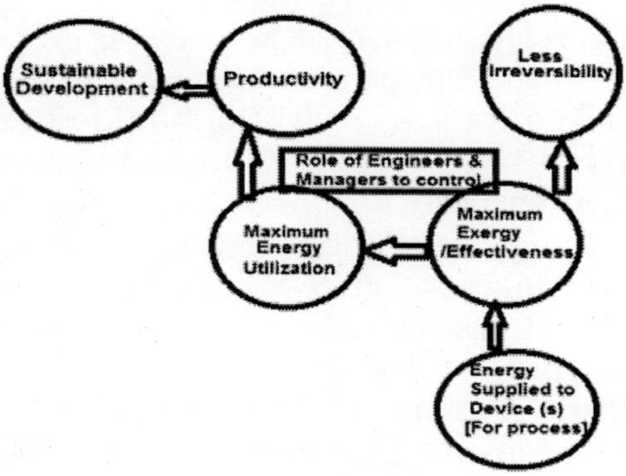

Management in Services and Manufacturing Unit

Every processing organizerproduces some physical goods. Here, operational management or transformation management plays the role. Aziz et al.[6] (2014) indicated about OprMAS (Operating Procedures Management System) for plant processing system. According to them there are nine interfaces that follow the OP framework. They are: Development of operating procedures, initial start-up, normal operation, temporary operation, emergency operation, emergency shutdown, normal shutdown and normal shutdown after emergency shutdown and then start-up and safe practices. Therefore, a systematic method of processing by a smooth management of OP can solve to increase exergy; hence evolution of useful work and finally sustainable development is possible. Wang and Strong[7] (1996) pointed out about the recording of processing data in data computer system (DCS) and analyzed the data with quick response signal. According to Thomaset al.[8] (2004), Supervisory Control and Data Acquisition (SCADA) Laboratory facility must be implemented in processing plant. There must be three stations are to be introduced for a processing unit viz. Engineering stations, Operator stations and Application stations. These stations can function cumulatively to run a smooth productivity with less heat and work loss. Plant diagnostics (PD) and integration are often referred as applications. PD signifies smarter looking about what happens inside the plant during production. Barker and Frolick[9] (2003) highlighted about the integration of control system (batch) in production management and Enterprise Resource Planning (ERP) systems. In a processing (say, Food) plant General recipe (raw materials), Formulation of raw materials, Process and Batch control systems are directly connected with Laboratory Information Management system (LIMS). Material management is connected with General recipe / raw materials requirement. Ultimate capacity of plant. For operational process data a historian software is used which can collect data from process control system and finally fed to ERS systems for final corrected data input to run the plant smoothly. All are represented in Figure 2.

Figure 2: ERP system and operational systems connected with Historian Software.

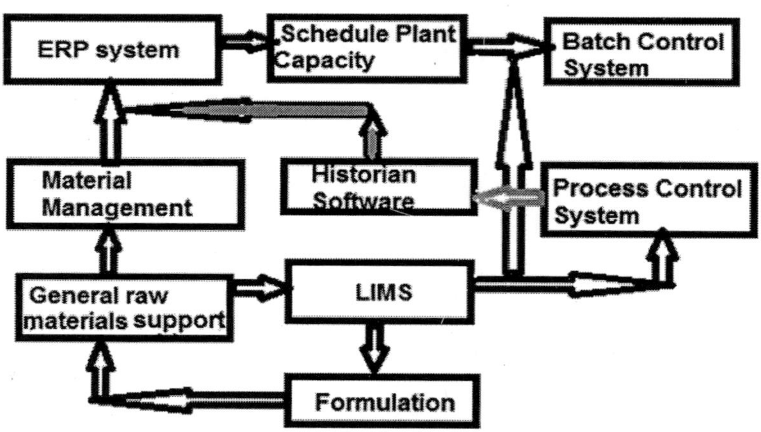

Many processing unit already implemented ERP / MRP[10] systems with the intension of achieving control over their global product supply mechanism. The main advantage for this system is to standardize the data models to permit the standardization in plant processing.

For the food processing plant the quality parameters to be maintained for the finished product. Therefore, a controlling aspect on handling critical control parameters (CCP) and HACCP analysis to be maintained on line processing keeping in mind on development of more exergy efficiency which can directly associated with the process operation with almost zero environmental impact. The reason behind that the exergy is only converted from one form to another formwithout any loss.

Conclusion

From the day of human life beginning in this world they were eager to develop their life style from the first firing to the journey into space. Modern civilization is now busy for searching alternative sources of energy. But people forget to use energy judiciously. A balance is to be needed between the correct use and generation of energy. Use of more efficient available energy (exergy) with minimum work lost (due to irreversibility) is utmost requirement for survival of human life. That is why the term "sustainable development" implemented in modern science and management. Keeping in mind to draw a parallel line between the more productivity and less irreversibility is our destination. Science and technology is blessing only if they are used for constructive roots with less bad impact on environment.

REFERENCES

1. Industrial Development for the 21st Century: Sustainable Development Perspectives. Department of Economic and Social Affairs (DESA). United Nations, New York, 2007.
2. Demirel, Y. 2006, International Journal of Exergy, vol. 3, p. 345-361.

3. Moran, M.S., and H.N. Shapiro. 2012. Fundamentals of Engineering Thermodynamics, 7thEdn., John Wiley and Sons, NY.

4. VAN Wylen, G.J.,and Sonntag, R.E. 1985. Fundamentals of Classical Thermodynamics, 3rdEdn., John Wiley and Sons, New York.

5. Mintzberg, H. 1973. The nature of Managerial Work, 2ndEdn.,Harper & Row, New York.

6. Aziz, M.M.A., Hainin, M.R., Yaacob, H., Ali, Z., Chang, F.-L., and Adnan, A. 2014.Characterization and Utilization of Steel Slag for the Construction of Roads and Highways.Materials Research Innovations.DOI 10.1179 / 1432891714 z. 0000000000967.

7. Wang, R.Y., and Strong, D.M. 1996. Beyond Accuracy: What Data Quality Means to Data Consumers. Journal of Management Information Systems, Springer, vol. 12 (4), p. 5-34.

8. Thomas, M.S., Kumar, P., and Chandna, V. K. 2004. Design, Development, and Commissioning of a Supervisory Control and Data Acquisition (SCADA) Laboratory for Research and Training.IEEE Transactions of Power Systems, vol. 19 (3), p. 1582-1588.

9. Barker, T., and Frolick, M.N. 2003. Erp implementation Failure: a case study. Information Systems Management, vol. 20 (4), 43-49.

10. Daniel, J.B., and Chan, K.H. 1989. Materials Requirements Planning and Purchasing. Journal of Purchasing & Material Management, vol. 25 (1), p. 1-6.

14

A Review of Literature on the Factors Plaguing the Healthcare Management System of West Bengal, India

Satakshi Chatterjee

ABSTRACT

Health is considered to be a basic necessity of the common people. Every citizen of India has a right to receive best healthcare services in order to maintain optimal health. The healthcare sector has a huge role in this arena. The healthcare management system takes into account all the issues and challenges of the healthcare system and analyses the data. The objective of this paper is to look at all the factors that directly or indirectly affect the healthcare management system of West Bengal. The data is obtained from all the existing literature pertaining to this specific area. The three determinants which were seen to play a significant role in this aspect are the lack of accessibility to healthcare services and financial instability, inefficient functioning of the healthcare providers and a decrease in the satisfaction of the patients. The factors need to be addressed immediately and a short term solution could be devised in terms of Public Private Partnerships.

Keywords: Healthcare, Healthcare management system, Accessibility, Patient Satisfaction.

Introduction

Health is considered as one of the most important needs of mankind. As per World Health Organisation, "Health is defined as a state of complete, physical, mental and social well being and not merely the absence of disease or infirmity". Healthy people also generate good quality work which increases the productivity of the organisations drastically. Thus, it has an indirect impact on the growth of the nation's economy as well.

The healthcare sector plays a crucial role in providing good health services to all citizens. This responsibility is of the government of India as per the Constitution of India (Bajpai, et al., 2005). Primary health care services must be available to each and every citizen of India. However, the accessibility of this service across each and every part of India is a big challenge for the government. Thus, the Twelfth year plan has given this issue an utmost priority level. The aim of this project is to offer faster, sustainable and superior inclusive growth.

There is an existence of a huge lacuna in the public healthcare sector. As a result, the general mass is forced to seek healthcare services from the private healthcare sector as even though it is much more expensive (Raman, et al., 2012). India is a nation which has got one of the most highest out of pocket expenses in the private healthcare sector. This is because of the reason that health insurance is not provided to each and every citizen of India by the government. As a result, the general population could afford healthcare services according to their income level. The merits of health insurance are becoming more and more evident to the people and that is why all brackets of people are looking to adopt this in the long run.

Several nations have considered a partnership with certain non-governmental entities to increase the efficiency of the healthcare services. India is one of the nations which give these public private partnerships huge importance. However, this is not a permanent solution for the developing countries or undeveloped nations. This is especially so as because these countries are responsible for providing uniform healthcare services to all the needy people irrespective of their income level (Kumar, et al., 2011). One of the reasons for this insufficient healthcare provision is that of the issue of availability of the required funding from the central government. It has also been seen from various studies and reports that the expenditure of the Indian government on healthcare sector is much lower than the actual requirement (Rao, et al., 2012).

West Bengal is a state which has a very high population density as compared to most other states of India because of its geographical location. However, a huge disparity has been observed in the consumption of the services related to healthcare in the urban and the rural regions. There is the existence of a huge disparity between the various districts of West Bengal based on the accessibility, usability as well as availability of the healthcare services. All these factors are inversely related to the per capita district domestic product of West Bengal (Chatterjee, et al., 2013). This paper aims at taking a look at the factors related to the management system of the healthcare sector which play a key role in the proliferation of these issues.

Literature Review

Healthcare management system is a common subject amongst researchers nowadays. As a result, various theoretical as well as empirical studies have been carried in this subject. Some of the factors pertaining to healthcare management system have been found in the existing literature. These factors could be broadly classified under three segments: accessibility and financing of healthcare services, efficiency of the healthcare sector and the perception of patients towards healthcare services. All of these factors have been highlighted below.

One of the fundamental activities of the healthcare management system is the improvement of the accessibility of healthcare. In the context of healthcare, access for particular healthcare services is defined as the access to a particular healthcare service which is given to the customers by the help of a provider or an organisation. This concept of accessibility of healthcare services is multi faceted and different authors have different perceptions about this particular topic.

Some studies suggest that accessibility is the core of healthcare management systems. It is responsible for recognising the needs of the people and accordingly, it helps them in the search of the suitable healthcare facilities (Levesque, et al., 2013). Other studies showcase that physical accessibility as well as financial accessibility work in tandem to define accessibility towards a particular healthcare service (Salkever, 1976). Other authors have given five factors to suitability describe accessibility and they are physical ease of use, excellence, user-friendliness of the monetary issues, availability as well as suitability (Peters, et al., 2007).

Very strong disparities have been found in the accessibility of the healthcare services in the rural areas as compared to the urban areas (Lamiraud, et al., 2005). It has been seen that the rural population is much more dependent on the healthcare services provided by the public sector as compared to the urban population. Certain remote areas are there which have got no access to healthcare services all together. A patient has to travel hundreds of kilometres in order to reach the nearest healthcare centre to receive treatment. Hence, it is very difficult to get the treatment on time and in one out of five cases, the situation becomes fatal for the patients. Hence, majority of the people in these areas have to depend on herbal remedies for their problems, which, many a mes, become ineffective.

The key objective of a healthcare management system to provide equal healthcare services to all the citizens a nation as it is their fundamental right. In this manner, the patients will not have any financial burden and will be able to receive treatment for their ailment (Mikkonen, et al., 2010). This scheme will be particularly useful to those citizens who belong to the lower income bracket of the society. They cannot afford the cost of the healthcare services needed by them and this is especially true in case of the private healthcare service provider. Hence, they are forced to forego their treatment for their inability to pay. Healthcare management systems should look into this issue and uproot this problem from its very foundation.

Another big obstacle in the functioning of the management system is the inadequate number of doctors. There are many primary healthcare units which are operating without the presence of a qualified doctor (Birbeck, et al., 2002). As a result, complete healthcare coverage needs vigorous work with support from the government. Financing this complete healthcare coverage is a long term plan and it will need intense planning and careful implementation. However, if it is done in the right manner, then it can be done without any hitches. In the short run, accessibility needs to be increased as much as possible through the public private partnerships so that the basic primary health services are available to all.

There is a scarcity of resources in the healthcare sector. As a result, the efficient and judicial use of the human as well as the financial resources becomes very important. Some methods must be developed in order to measure the efficiency of the healthcare facilities as a whole. This would ensure that the policy makers would be able to devise certain methods to optimally utilise these resources (Jat, et al., 2013). Countries who have implemented this have shown remarkable results in terms of receptiveness, upgraded healthcare status as well as equality in the financing of healthcare services.

It is not very easy to measure the efficiency of the healthcare service providers, mainly hospitals. However, the measurement of the efficiency can be made possible by considering the different types of management styles implemented in the different hospitals. Data envelopment analysis has been used in the assessment of the efficiency issues of various hospitals (Worthington, 2004). Various challenges are there in the usage of this particular method. A minute alteration in the collection of the data could result in hugely dissimilar data. The only way out of this is to measure the comparative technical efficiency and the scale efficiency of the people (Osei, et al., 2005).

Patients are the main determinants who can gauge the quality of the services offered by the service provider. That is why various studies are carried out which have tried to determine the satisfaction index of the patients (Yadav, 2007).Patients residing in the rural belt tend to visit the public hospitals whereas the patients residing in the urban belt prefer the private hospitals. Also, patients generally prefer to visit larger hospitals which are located nearby and have a big infrastructure. This inspires confidence in the minds of the people. The type of ailment of the patient also significantly affects the choice of the hospitals.

There is a perception that the rural hospitals and the small urban hospitals provide inferior quality services. As a result, they tend to avoid these hospitals if any alternative is available in the long run. Also, the patients can also be admitted to the various hospitals based on their health insurance coverage (Dranove, et al., 1993). In spite of all these, patients are likely to switch hospitals if the doctors refer them to a particular hospital which is known for a particular service which the patient needs immediately. This is an unique point of this industry as health needs are necessary to fulfil for the survival of the individuals. Thus, these factors were some of the points which are crucial to the functioning of the healthcare management system.

Discussion

The Millennium Development Goals have targeted

the elimination of poverty and the enhancement of the healthcare services. However, India has a long way to go before reaching this goal. West Bengal can be considered as a commonly superior state of India as compared to its average, however, the issues and challenges in the healthcare sector need to be identified and addressed. All the significant issues of the healthcare management system which is in lace need to be analysed carefully and the problem areas need to be identified. Remedial medical services should be made accessible to all at a relatively affordable cost. The morbidity as well as the mortality rate of the general public must be reduced.

The pressure on the medical professionals in government hospitals is very high as majority of the population seek healthcare service from the government hospitals, especially, inpatient service. Better regulation on the part of the government is the need of the hour. There is a very distinct gap in the hospital infrastructure as well in the district level (Sheet, et al., 2013). On top of this, the various healthcare units do not operate to their optimal level, thus, wasting the precious resources.

To tackle the inadequacies of the government pertaining to the healthcare services, the government is going for various Public Private Partnership models to increase the accessibility of the healthcare services of the common people. This ensures that the common people will be able to get the basic healthcare service facilities which must be available to all. The out of pocket expenditure of the patients also comes down drastically as the services are provided at a basic rate.

Conclusion

This paper showcases that a number of studies have been conducted to gather information about the current healthcare management system of West Bengal, India. Various government reports have also been generated with various institutional initiatives. These reports are a rich source of information about the current state of the healthcare service providers of India.

Accessibility of the healthcare services to the common people is a major problem which is reflected from the various research papers. There is a huge out of pocket expenditure in case the patient seeks treatment from a private healthcare provider. As a result, majority of the people could not afford this and seeks treatment from public healthcare provider. This puts an immense pressure on the government as there are certain infrastructural limitations as well as an inadequate number of doctors. All these factors lead to the inefficient operation of the hospitals which brings down its quality index. As a result, the satisfaction of the patients also decreases.

The need of the hour a complete analysis of the total healthcare infrastructure and devising plans to optimally utilise the human as well as the financial resources already present. This would lead to a marked increase in the efficiency of the hospitals which would further lead to an increase the patient satisfaction index. This would be a very complicated process as a huge number of factors is at play. However, through proper planning, it can be done and it will be a huge benefit to the society if the planning is properly implemented.

REFERENCES

1. Bajpai, N., Dholakia, R. H., & Sachs, J. D. (2005). *Scaling Up Primary Healthcare Services in Rural India: Public Investment Requirements and Health Sector Reform in MP and UP* (CGSD Working Paper 29). The Earth Institute at Columbia University, New York.

2. Raman, A. V. &Björkman, J. W. (2012). *Public-Private Partnership in Healthcare Delivery: Context, Outcome and Lessons in India.* Paper presented at 13th Winelands Conference on Public Administration, University of Stellenbosh, Republic of South Africa. Paper retrieved 02.10.2012 from ht:p:// www.deloitte.com/assets/Dcom-southAfrica/ Local%20Assets/Documents/ public_private_partnership_in_health_care_delivery_context.pdf.

3. Kumar, C., and Prakash, R. (2011). Public-Private Dichotomy in Utilization of Health Care Services in India. *The journal of Sustainable Development, 5(01),* 25-52.
4. Rao, M. G., Choudhury, M. (2012). *Health Care Financing Reforms in India* (Working Paper). Retrieved from National Institute of Public Finance and Policy website: http://www.nipfp.org.in/media/medialibrary/2013/04/wp_2012_100.pdf (15.12.13).
5. Chatterjee, S., Laha, A., &Sarkhel, J. (2013). Measuring Public Healthcare Access on West Bengal: Toward a Comprehensive Index (Ed.), *Challenges of Livelihood and Inclusive Rural Development in the Era of Globalization* (pp.279-292). New Delhi: New Delhi Publishers.
6. Levesque, J. F., Harris, M. F., & Russell, G. (2013). Patient-centred access to health care: conceptualising access at the interface of health systems and populations, International Journal for Equity in Health, 12 (18), Retrieved 06.07.14 from http://www.equityhealthj.com/content/12/1/18.
7. Salkever, D. S. (1976). Accessibility and the demand for preventive care. *Social Science Medicine, 10,* 469-475.
8. Peters, D. H., Garg, A., Bloom, G., Walker, D. G., Brieger, W. R., & Rahman, M. H. (2007). Poverty and access to health care in developing countries. *Annals of the New York Academic Sciences, 1136,* 161-171.
9. Lamiraud, K., Booysen, F., & Scheil-Adlung, X. (2005). The Impact of Social Health Protection on Access to Health Care, Health Expenditure and Impoverishment: A Case Study of South Africa. Retrieved from International Labor office, Geneva website: http://www.ilo.org/wcmsp5/groups/public/—ed_protect/—soc_sec/documents/publication/wcms_207709.pdf.
10. Mikkonen, J., & Raphael, D. (2010). *Social Determinants of Health: The Canadian Facts*. Retrieved 05.04.13 from http://www.thecanadianfacts.org/The_Canadian_Facts.pdf.
11. Birbeck, G. L., &Munsat, T. (2002). Neurologic Services in Sub-Saharan Africa: A Case Study Among Zambian Primary Healthcare Workers. *Journal of Neurological Sciences, 200*(1/2), 75-79.
12. Jat, T. R., & Sebastian, M. S. (2013). Technical efficiency of public district hospitals in Madhya Pradesh, India: a data envelopment analysis. *Global Health Action, 6 (10)*. Retrieved

15.02.2013 from http://dx.doi.org/10.3402/gha.v6i0.21742.

13. Worthington, A. C. (2004). Frontier Efficiency Measurement in Health Care: A Review of Empirical Techniques and Selected Applications. Medical Care Research and Review. 61(2), 135-170.
14. Osei, D., d'Almeida, S., George, M. O., Kirigia, J. M., Mensah, A. O., &Kainyu, L. H. (2005). Technical efficiency of public district hospitals and health centres in Ghana: a pilot study. *Cost Effectiveness and Resource Allocation, 3(9).* Retrieved 22.12.2013 from http://www.resource-allocation.com/content/3/1/9.
15. Yadav, J. U. (2007). Reasons for choosing a government hospital for treatment. *Indian Journal of Community Medicine, 32(3),* 235-236.
16. Dranove, D., White, W. D., and Wu, L. (1993). Segmentation in local Hospital markets. *Medical Care, 31(1),* 52-64.
17. Sheet, S., Roy, T. (2013). A Micro Level Analysis of Disparities in Health Care Infrastructure in Birbhum District, West Bengal, India. *IOSR Journal of Humanities and Social Science (IOSR-JHSS), 7(3),* 25-31.

15

Cross Sectional Study of Impact of Literacy Rate on Crime Against Indian Women

Dr. Jayeeta Majumder & Dr. Sourav Gangopadhyay

ABSTRACT

The literacy rate in India is increasing day by day. Literacy has positive impact on growth of country. Literacy makes people aware, knowledgeable; it minimizes the barrier of cast, race, religion and many others. Many researchers have shown literacy is able to minimize the crime rate, but many of them doubted that literacy is nothing to do with crime. Crime against women is persisting in our countries. To see whether the literacy is able to minimize the crime against women we have collected secondary data from handbook of statistics on Indian states Published by Reserve Bank of India and crime in India 2016 published by National Crime Records Bureau. In those areas literacy rate and the crime rate of 28 numbers of states are collected. To see whether the crime against women is depending upon the literacy, we have done ANOVA by the help of SPSS 17th version. The result shows that the literacy is not able to create statically significant difference among the states of high literacy and states of low literacy. So literacy is nothing to do with crime against women in Indian context.

Keyword: literacy, crime, women, ANOVA, Reserve Bank of India, National Crime Record Bureau

Introduction

Many research paper shows that the Crime against women and children is associated with the literacy but the crime against women and children is also related with several other factors which are complex in nature (Deyessa, 2010). In India the women populations are soft target, in this regard many states of India has organized literacy program to deal with it (Ropmay, 2014). Many study shows that the illiterate women are more vulnerable to be harassed. Illiterate women are abused twice more than literate women (Raya, 2012; Chadha, 2018). Literacy provides the opportunities to grow awareness, empowerments of women and it enhances the social awareness, girl enrolments, gender equity and many more (Singh, 2015), literacy reduces the risk of crime against women (Hadi, 2010) but many study shows different results like A study shows in Kerala crime against women is increasing day by even though Kerala is having highest literacy rate.The education and the literacy are not being able to change the violence against women and children (Nithya, 2013). After reviewing some research papers it was decided to analyze whether there is any relation is existed between adult literacy and crime against women. Some paper suggested that Indian literacy rate is increasing day by day but the crime against women population is remaining same (Hossain, 2016).

Study Design

Cross sectional Secondary Data analysis has done, the secondary dataare collected from Different Website. Like Literacy Rate of allstates of India in the year 2016, were collected from handbook of statistics on Indian states Published by Reserve Bank of India. The crime against women is collected from crime in India 2016 published by National Crime Records Bureau.

Sample Size

Total 28 states of India are included in the study. The name of the states are - Andhra Pradesh, Arunachal Pradesh, Assam, Bihar, Chhattisgarh, Goa, Gujarat, Haryana, Himachal Pradesh , Jammu and Kashmir, Jharkhand, Karnataka, Kerala, Madhya Pradesh, Maharashtra, Manipur, Meghalaya, Mizoram, Nagaland, Odisha, Punjab, Rajasthan, Sikkim, Tamil Nadu, Tripura, Uttar Pradesh, Uttarakhand and West Bengal

Settings

Literacy rate and crime against women rate of 28 states are collected. 28 states are divided into two groups in respect of literacy rate. The average literacy rate of the entire country is 74.04. In the first group 17 states included where the literacy is more than the entire country's literacy rate i.e. 74.04 and incase of second group where rest of the states are included i.e. 11 number of states, and all are having below 74.04% of literacy rate. After that number of crime against women during the year 2016 is collected.

Variables

Two variables are taken in the study- literacy rate and number of crime committed against women population.

Data Analysis

To see whether there is any difference of crime rate against women between two groups of states, or we can say whether crime against women is depending upon the literacy rate of the state, we ran ANOVA by using SPSS soft ware 17th version. The result of the

Result

The table 1 is showing the literacy rate and the crime against women rate of 29 states of India. The table is also showing 29 states are divided into two groups.

The following table is showing that 28 states are divided into two groups first group is containing those states where the literacy rate is lower than the national mean of literacy whereas the second group is containing those states which are having higher literacy rate than the national literacy rate. The national literacy rate of 2016 is 74.04 %. The state having lowest literacy is Bihar having 63.82% and the state having highest literacy rate is Kerala having 93.91 % literacy rate. Apart from that, Utter Pradesh having highest number of reported crime rate against women which is 49262 and whereas Mizoram is having only 120 reported crime rate against women which is considered lowest among 28 states.Now it is to see whether literacy is playing a significant role in crime against women or not. ANOVA is run and the descriptive analysis is showing the following result.

Table 1 Literacy rate and Reported crime rate against women

Types of States	*Name of the States*	*Literacy*	*Crime Against Women*
States having lower literacy rate than national mean literacy rate	Andhra Pradesh	67.66	16362
	Arunachal Pradesh	66.95	367
	Assam	73.18	20869
	Bihar	63.82	13400
	Chhattisgarh	71.04	5947
	Jammu and Kashmir	68.74	2850
	Jharkhand	67.63	5453
	Madhya Pradesh	70.63	26604
	Odisha	73.45	17837
	Rajasthan	67.06	27422
	Uttar Pradesh	69.72	49262
States having higher literacy rate than national mean literacy rate	Goa	87.40	371
	Gujarat	79.31	8532
	Haryana	76.64	9839
	Himachal Pradesh	83.78	1222
	Karnataka	75.60	14131
	Kerala	93.91	10034

Maharashtra	82.91	31388
Manipur	79.85	253
Meghalaya	75.48	372
Mizoram	91.58	120
Nagaland	80.11	105
Punjab	76.68	5105
Sikkim	82.20	153
Tamil Nadu	80.33	4463
Tripura	87.75	1013
Uttarakhand	79.63	1588
West Bengal	77.08	32513

Table 2: Descriptive analysis

	N	*Mean of reported crime against women*
States having Less than National literacy Mean	17	11341.88
States having more than National literacy Mean	11	10433
Total	28	10984.82

From the above chart it can be concluded that the mean of reported crime against women in those states whereliteracy rateis lesser than national literacy mean(11341.88) and the mean of reported crime against women in thosestates having more literacy rate than National literacy mean(10433). Apart from that it can be concluded that the mean of reported crime against women in those states having less than national literacy mean, is higher than those states where literacy mean is higher than national mean. That means reported crime against women is lower in case of those states where literacy rate is higher that national literacy mean. Now it is to see whether the difference is statistically significant or not, ANOVA ran and the ANOVA table shows the result as below.

Table 3: ANOVA table

	Sum of Squares	*Df*	*Mean Square*	*F*	*Significance*
Between Groups	5516948.342	1	5516948.342	.033	.857
Within Groups	4.340E9	26	1.669E8		
Total	4.346E9	27			

From the first ANOVA table, it can be concluded that there is no significant differences persisting among two groups states on existing mean of reported crime against women. F (1, 26) =.033, and the significant value is .857, which is greater than .005 and which is insignificant.

Discussion:

So it can be concluded that the differences of mean of reported crime against women of states having higher literacy and states having lower literacy, is not statistically significant. So it means literacy is not playing a role in reported crime rate against women in India. Though many researchers have shown opposite regulates but there are number of researches have conducted which is showing the same result as this article is showing. Crime against women is caused by several factors; social, political, psychological and many other factors are responsible for it. Only improving the literacy rate, is not able to improve the situation. Literacy could be an important element to improve many situations including crime against women but without addressing other factors crime against women will not be controlled.

Conclusion

Increasing rate of crime against women is a sham for any country. It is related with several factors. Literacy is among them but this is not the only cause. We need to analyze the literacy rate of different groups according to gender, age, relatives, religion and many more. We need to see how they are creating impact on the crime rate against women. We need to see other factors apart from literacy such as social, political and many more, to see how those factors are related with the crime rate against women. This article is only concentrated on the overall literacy rate and the reported crime against women. There are many crimes are committed against women who are not reported, we should also think about that.

REFERENCES

1. Hadi ST (2010). The Face of Intimate Partner Violence in Bangladesh: Revealing Patterns from the Existing Literature. Bangladesh e-Journal of Sociology 7: 12-20.
2. Brahmapurkar, K. P. (2017). Gender equality in India hit by illiteracy, child marriages and violence: a hurdle for sustainable development. *Pan African Medical Journal*, 28(178). DOI:10.11604/pamj.2017.28.178.13993
3. Chadha, N. and Wadhwa, S. Impact of an Adult Literacy Programmeon the Personal and Public Lives of Women: Evidence from India. *Journal of South Asian Development*, 13(1). 82-111. DOI: 10.1177/0973174118764930
4. Deyessa, N.; Berhane, Y.; Ellsberg, M.; Emmelin, M.; Kullgren, G.andHogberg, U. (2010). Violence against women in relation to literacy and area of residence in Ethiopia. *Global Health Action*, 3(2070). 1-9. DOI: 10.3402/gha.v3i0.2070
5. Hossain, A. (2016). The Impact of Domestic Violence on Women: A Case Study of Rural Bangladesh. *Social Crimonol*, 4(1), 1-8. DOI:10.4172/2375-4435.1000135
6. Nithya, N.R. (2013). High Literacy and Mounting Violence: A Case of Women in Kerala, India. *International Journal of Scientific and Research Publications*, 3(9). 1-9.
7. Ropmay, A.D. (2014). Crimes against Women in Matrilineal Meghalaya A Forensic Medical Perspective. *J Indian Acad Forensic Med*, 36(4). 399-403.
8. Singh, C.K. (2015). Womens Literacy in India- Issues and Challenges. *Global Journal of Interdesciplinary Social Sciences*, 4(4), 41-44.

16

Demystifying the Insolvency and Bankruptcy Code in the Indian Context

Asmita Basu

ABSTRACT

Bankruptcy is used for the formal procedure for individuals (not companies in many countries) who are declared by law to be insolvent. In the situation of insolvency, to solve the problem of NPA, make the exit process easier for the investors and also to attract fresh capital and foreign investors, a new legislative framework has been evolved known as Insolvency and Bankruptcy Code, 2016 (IBC). IBC, 2016 was passed by the Parliament on 11th May 2016, received Presidential assent on 28th May, 2016. IBC is the only bankruptcy law of India which seeks to consolidate the existing framework by creating a single law for insolvency and bankruptcy. The present research paper aims to highlight the features of this new law and its various scopes and prospects in the Indian context. It also focuses on the Insolvency and Bankruptcy Codes which have been prevalent in other countries like UK and US long before its introduction in India.

Key Words: Insolvency, Bankruptcy, Law

Introduction

Many a times a company may not have enough assets

to cover its debts and/or it cannot pay its debt on the due date, then the company is called insolvent. "Insolvency" means inability to pay debts as they fall due- from the Latin word *"solvere"* to pay. Bankruptcy is collective procedure for recovery of debts by creditors (Wood,2007)[1]. Bankruptcy is used for the formal procedure for individuals (not companies in many countries) who are declared by law to be insolvent.Liquidation means turning a company's assets into cash and then distributing this to the creditors. The most commonly used procedure for insolvent companies; liquidation is the end of the road. After the assets are sold and the proceeds distributed, the company is struck off the register, or dissolved.

Post-independence the industrial policies in India, such as import substitution, industrial licensing, and limited private ownership, promoted a group of inefficient and uncompetitive companies. Due to deregulation, foreign competition and financial reform a number of financially unviable firms had to consider exit or restructuring options. However, the existing legal, political and social system did not provide the appropriate framework for efficient and equitable resolution of insolvency cases, thus dramatically slowing down the pace of the much needed industrial restructuring. Till very recently there was no single comprehensive and integrated policy on corporate bankruptcy in India. Previously there used to be different legislative acts and special provisions, which used to provide procedural guidance on the liquidation or reorganization process and there was an involvement of different agencies, having overlapping jurisdiction, which used to create systemic delays and complexities in the process. The main objective of a well-functioning bankruptcy system is to promote economic efficiency by maximizing the total value of assets, the Indian system fails, as under this system, liquidation or reorganization is extremely time and resource costly; the system does not encourage optimal valuation outcomes; and creates incentives for managers or stockholders to take actions that generate private benefits at the expense of firm value.In the situation of insolvency, to solve the problem of Non-Performing Assets (NPA) has been the main objective for the development and formulation of the Insolvency and Bankruptcy code (IBC) in India.

Insolvency and Bankruptcy Code in other countries:

In the bankruptcy process efficiency of an organizationcan be measuredin three stages -ex ante, interim, and ex post- which depend particularly on the information available at the time. Holmstrom and Myerson (1983)[2], have define the three stages asthe ex-ante stage is the time before any private information is received by any individual; the interim stage is when private information has been received, but it has not been shared amongst others; and, ultimately, the ex post stage is when each and every private information is common knowledge for all. Since the integrated form of Insolvency and Bankruptcy Code in India is a newly launched concept, we must focus on some other countries where this regulation has got considerable amount of history. The Insolvency and Bankruptcy Codesof the two important countries that have been studied as part of the present study are UK and US.

Insolvency Code in UK

During the process of insolvency in UK, prior to the 1986 Insolvency Act, formal reorganization of any company wasmediated by the three possible routes to: 1) liquidation, 2) receivership, and 3) company voluntary arrangements. An additional procedure, administration, was introduced in 1986. The most widely used course of action is the liquidation code, which accounted for about three quarters of all formal reorganizations since 1990, while further 22% was accounted for receivership (Rajak, 1994)[3].

The main objective of the liquidator is to sell the requisite amount of assets of the firm to repay creditors. The liquidator may sell the company as a going concern or in a non- operating state, but if he uses funds belonging to creditors to delay the sale, then he would risk dismissal or legal action. If one or more of the firm's creditors have a particular kind of lien on the firm's assets then it can lead to Receivership. This is known as a floating charge, which is a claim on moveable assets such as stocks and work in progress. The creditor appoints the receiverwith the floating charge, and he represents the interests of that particular creditor only with virtually no duty of care towards other creditors. The powers of the receiver are significant (Franks et al, 1996)[4].

Bankruptcy Code in US

The Bankruptcy code in US is an integrated regulation. It holds two main bankruptcy procedures for the US corporations: Chapter 7 and Chapter 11. Chapter 7 denotes the liquidation provision. It provides for the scope of appointing a trustee by the court to oversee the entire process of liquidation of the company. Inevitably during the liquidation procedure, the firm is closed down prior to sale and its assets are auctioned. Chapter 11 essentially allows a firm to continue its operation on one hand while on the other a plan of reorganization is worked out with its creditors. To facilitate this process, the directors of the corporation are further permitted to stay in charge also providing substantial rights to the firm, which is often referred to as the debtor-in-possession.

In majority of the cases, the existing management remains in control, while new management is appointed in the large number of remaining cases (Gilson, 1989)[5]. In some cases, the court may appoint a trustee. Appointing a trustee is generally a temporary measure until new management is appointed. Most of the firms enter Chapter 11 only after attempting to resolve through an informal reorganization or workout outside of the bankruptcy process.The reason behind this is primarily the cost and the time involved in Chapter 11 procedure is huge in comparison to the procedures of workout (Franks and Torous, 1994)[6].

Background for the development of IBC

The ability to liquidate totally unviable Indian firms rapidly has often compelled creditors to support going-concern restructuring when they should have cut their losses and forced these companies to wind-up" (Goswami, 1996)[7]. Initiallythere was no single comprehensive and integrated policy oncorporate bankruptcy in India comparable with the bankruptcy code in the US or UK which have a structured framework. There were three major legislativeActs and several special provisions, which used to provide procedural guidanceon the liquidation or reorganization process. As a result, four differentagencies, the High Courts, the Company Law Board, the Board forIndustrial and Financial Reconstruction (BIFR), and the Debt RecoveryTribunals (DRTs), have been coinciding with one another's jurisdiction, leading toslow down of the entire system and bringing in complexities in the process (Kang &Nayar, 2004)[8]. The key legislations, regulations and non-statutory guidance amended aresummarized below, which were previously followed by an assessment and implications for thecompanies in financial distress, namely-

- Companies Act 1956/ 2013
- Securitization& Reconstruction of Financial Assets and Enforcement of Security Interest Act, 2002 (SARFAESI Act, 2002),
- Recovery of Debts Due to Banks and Financial Institutions Act, 1993 , (RDDBFI Act, 1993),
- Sick Industrial Companies Act, 1985 (SICA Act, 1985),
- Other enactments for partnership and individual insolvencies,

- Non-statutory guidelines/ out of court mechanism

Insolvency and Bankruptcy Code- Implementation journey of the code:

The **Insolvency and Bankruptcy Code, 2016 (IBC)** was passed by the Parliament on 11th May 2016, received Presidential assent on 28th May, 2016. IBC was approved by both Houses of the Parliament and received the presidential assent in May 2016. It was made operational from 1st December 2016. IBC at present is touted as the second most important legislative reform (after GST) that has been initiated by the Government in order to resolve the NPA problem, make the exit process easier for investors, attract fresh capital and foreign investors. It will also target at channelizing capital to more productive assets and give a boost to India's ease of doing business.

IBC is the only bankruptcy law of India which seeks to consolidate the existing framework by creating a single law for insolvency and bankruptcy. The Code outlines separate insolvency resolution processes for individuals, companies and partnership firms. This law replaces Sick Industrial Companies (special provisions), Repeal Act, 2003 and amends other legislations like Companies Act, 2013, The Securitization and Reconstruction of Financial Assets and Enforcement of Security Interest Act, 2002 (also known as the **SARFAESI** Act), etc.. IBC will provide timely resolution process, bringing down drastically the time taken to wind up a sick company, initiating a swift process.

Objective section of the code

- Consolidate and amend laws relating to insolvency and bankruptcy
- Maximization of value
- Time-bound resolution
- Promote entrepreneurship and availability of credit

- Alteration of priority of payments of Government dues
- Establish an insolvency and bankruptcy board in India.

Insolvency and Bankruptcy Ecosystem

The following diagram shows the ecosystem and the participating organisations in the Insolvency regime.

IBBI- It is the apex body for promoting transparency & governance in the administration of the Code. It will be involved in setting up the infrastructure and accrediting Insolvency Professionals (IPs) & Information Utilities (IUs).

Information Utilities (IUs) - centralized repository of financial and credit information of borrowers. It would validate the information and claims of creditors as well as borrowers, as needed.

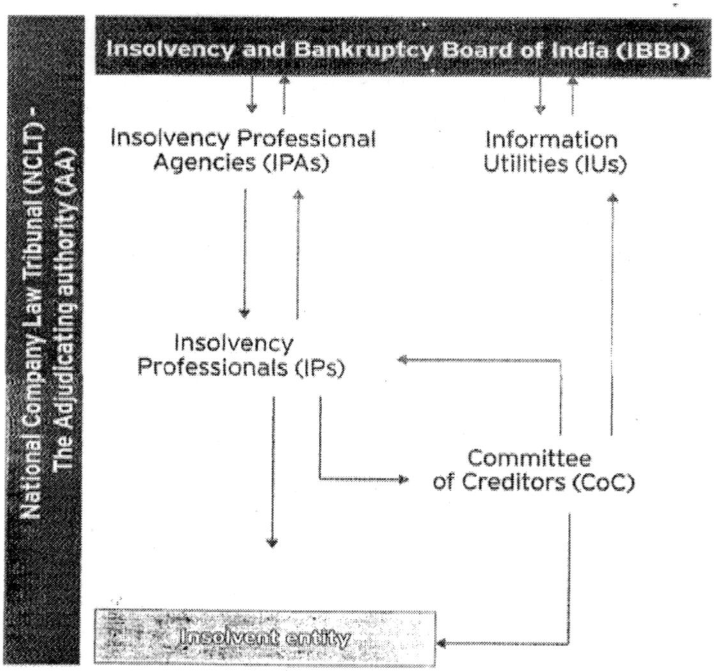

Insolvency Professional Agencies (IPAs) – These are professional bodies registered by the Board to promote and regulate the insolvency profession. These bodies will enrol IPs.

Insolvency Professionals (IPs)- They are licensed professionals regulated by the IBBI. The will conduct resolution process. They will act as Liquidator. They will be appointed by the creditors and will assume the powers of suspended board of directors.

The Adjudicating Authority (AA)- It would be National Company Law Tribunal (NCLT) for corporate insolvency. It will help to entertain or dispose any insolvency application, approve/ reject resolution plans, decide in respect of claims or matters of law / facts thereof.

Committee of Creditors (CoC)- It consists of financial creditors who will appoint and supervise actions of IPs and also focus on approval of the resolution plan.

Role and Responsibilities of IP under the code:

The key powers and duties of Resolution professionals are as follows:

- The powers of the board of directors of the corporate debtor, shall stand suspended and be exercised by the Interim Resolution Professional (IRP) / Insolvency Professional (IP).
- The officers and managers of the corporate debtor shall report to the IP and provides access to such documents and records of the corporate debtor as may be required.
- The IP shall act and execute in the name and on behalf of the corporate debtor all deeds, receipts and other documents.
- Collate all claims, from a Committee of Creditors (CoC), conduct the Corporate Insolvency Resolution Process (CIRP).

- Prepare the information memorandum (IM) and invite resolution plans.
- Investigate the official affairs of the company, appoint values.
- Take control and custody of any asset owned by the corporate debtor.

Corporate Insolvency Resolution Process (CIRP)

Default- Failure to pay whole or any part of instalment of the amount of debt or interest due (minimum INR 1 lakh).

Who can file the application?

- Financial Creditors
- Operational Creditors (including Government & employees / workmen)
- Corporate debtor
- No new application for CIRP can be made.

Interim Resolution Professional (IRP) / Resolution Professional (RP)

- Financial creditor and / or corporate applicant shall propose the name of an IRP in the application.
- It is optional for operational creditor to propose the name of an Interim IP.
- All powers of the suspended Board of Directors shall vest with the IRP / RP.
- RP is responsible to run the company as a going concern during CIRP.
- IRP / RP to get immunity from legal proceedings for action taken in good faith.

Moratorium

- The National Company Law Tribunal (NCLT) to declare moratorium from insolvency commencement date until completion of insolvency.

- Moratorium shall prohibit institution of suits, transfer of assets, foreclosure, recovery or enforcement under SARFAESI, recovery of assets.

Committee of Creditors (CoC)

- It consists of financial creditors only, excluding related parties.
- It includes secured and unsecured financial creditors
- It will confirm or replace IRP as RP
- It will approve several actions of RP

Resolution plan

The resolution plan must provide for

- Payment of insolvency resolution
- Process costs
- Repayment of the debt of operational creditors
- Management of affairs of the borrower after the plan is approved
- Implementation & supervision of the approved plan

Voting Power

- Only financial creditors have voting power in the committee in the ratio of debt owed
- All decision of the committee shall be approved by 75% of financial creditors
- Directors and operational creditors can attend the meeting, but would not have any voting rights

Fast Track Insolvency for debtors with

- Assets and income below a level
- Such class of creditors

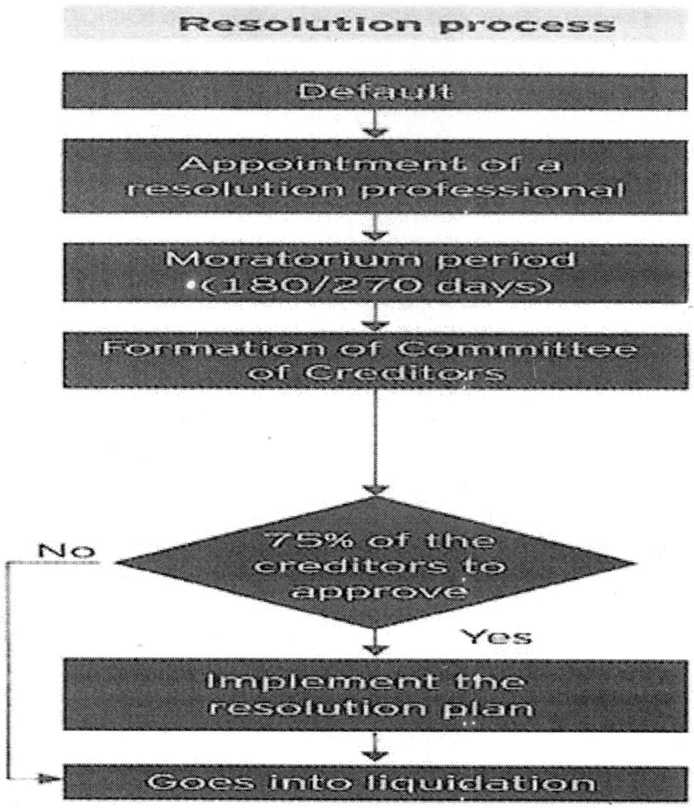

- Other categories as notified by the Central Government to be completed in 90 days, with a one-time extension of 45 days.

Conclusion

IBC has radically altered the insolvency law landscape in India. As evident from the present study that effectiveness of Insolvency code or Bankruptcy code in countries like UK and US is due to series of alterations and integration of regulations in this regard. In Indian context the first attempt to integrate the insolvency and bankruptcy laws and procedures will need to pass through the test of time.

Eventually the clear shift in the existing regulations will go a long way in resolving distressed situations, enhancing recoveries for all stakeholders reducing the scope for the wrongful exercise of legal authority by the directors to take creditor-focused action at the early stages of financial difficulty could create pitfalls for professional managers and directors who may not have any fraudulent or criminal intent. While the legal issues are expected to be ironed out over a period of time as the insolvency landscape matures, the other practical issues can only be handled by team effort, where each stakeholder works in unison, in the interest of collective resolution instead of serving individual interests. A creditor has an option of either insolvency tools to enforce recovery and/ or liquidation of the company or the bankruptcy of the individual. In many cases, this action can be counter-productive by forcing a business to cease trading and depressing the realizable value of the assets.

It is often preferable to ensure a business keeps trading to preserve value and future customers. This is dependent upon the directors co-operating in recognized financial difficulty and implementing a rescue procedure such as insolvency. This can require persuasion and negotiation with the creditor, who will sometimes use a threat to wind up the company as a lever. Significant value can be preserved even in distressed situations, if the lenders act swiftly with a clear intent. Indian economist Montek S. Ahluwalia is of the opinion that when reform goals are indicated only as a broad direction, with the precise end-point and pace of transition left unstated, opposition is minimized, and the government is given room to retreat if necessary (Ahluwalia, 2002)[9].IBC is thus a test of the collective resilience and maturity of the creditors, debtors, professionals and regulators combined together.

REFERENCES

1. Wood, P. R. (2007). *Principles of international insolvency*. 1(1). Sweet & Maxwell.

2. Holmström, B.& Myerson, R. B. (1983). Efficient and durable decision rules with incomplete information. *Econometrica: Journal of the Econometric Society*, 1799-1819.

3. Rajak, H. (1994). The Challenges of Commercial Reorganizations in Insolvency: Empirical Evidence from England. *Current Developments in International and Comparative Corporate Insolvency Law, Oxford*.

4. Franks, J. R.; Nyborg, K. G. & Torous, W. N. (1996). A comparison of US, UK, and German insolvency codes. *Financial Management*, 86-101.

5. Gilson, S. C. (1989). Management turnover and financial distress. *Journal of financial Economics*. *25*(2): 241-262.

6. Franks, J. R.&Torous, W. N. (1994). A comparison of financial recontracting in distressed exchanges and Chapter 11 reorganizations. *Journal of financial economics*. *35*(3): 349-370.

7. Goswami, O. (1996). *Corporate bankruptcy in India: a comparative perspective*. OECD Publishing.

8. Kang, N.&Nayar N. (2004). The evolution of corporate bankruptcy law in India. *Money and Finance*, (Oct. 2003–Mar. 2004). 37-58.

9. Ahluwalia, M. S. (2002). Economic reforms in India since 1991: Has gradualism worked? *Journal of Economic perspectives*. 16(3): 67-88.

17

Diversity in the Public Eye Prompting Change: Legitimacy or Challenge

Jyoti Kumari Pandit

ABSTRACT

This study will help the people to understand the benefits and challenges in details and to find more probable benefits and challenges in this concern. Diversity in society has benefits like encouraging innovation, higher quality proving its legitimacy and also has some factors that act as challenge like being ignored, unfairness, raising conflicts, misunderstandings etc. The purpose of this paper is to review various studies that highlight the challenges and benefits. By comparing both we get that diversity in itself is a challenge for the society which brings, measures the change and also suggests that we have to work harder to meet with these challenges.

Introduction

Society is becoming more diverse thanks to amongst other elements, increased cross border mobility, flexible gender roles, improved residing standards and individualization procedures. Diversity prevailing in society is the unique variations of every individual. Different human beings have distinct values, behaviors and approaches to life. Diversity, the idea saves us from unfair discrimination and enhances equality within every individual. We should always value- variations like ethnicity, age, race, way of life, sexual, orientation of physical incapacity and spiritual belief. By encouraging workforce to recognize cultural, social and linguistic variety will provide a clear idea about how to work with differences in the same environment.These opportunities should be contemplated so as to understand whether the society is benefitted or dissuaded.

Literature Review

According to (Miles Hewstone, Miguel R. Ramos; European Journal of Social Psychology 46(7)· September 2016) claimed that Demographic tendencies can monitor modern societies have turn out to be more and more diverse. Within the social sciences, those changes have been meditated in worries approximately the results of social range. Whilst early studies stated that diversity may also have terrible effects for societies and people. These inconsistent findings initiated a scholarly debate concerning the effect of unique forms of variety for a host of social results. It is now clear that the differences and consequences caused by it need to be fully understood. By focusing on special ranges of diversity (i.e., within the society and in companies), this studies additionally sheds light on the effectiveness of ideologies and rules for dealing with range.

The discussion about the consequences of range is truly diverse in itself, as it has been a multidisciplinary concern regarding selection of perspectives inside the social sciences.

According to Helen Eboh Cletus, Abubakar Umar (2018), Workplace Diversity (WPD) is a holistic idea that denotes the variations that exist among humans running inside a company. It describes the complex bodily, sociological or psychological attributes including gender, ethnicity, sexual orientation, religious or affairs of state that outline an individual or group. The results found out that diversity in the administrative center enhances the critical wondering, hassle-fixing, and employee expert skills. Furthermore, it allows corporations to attract talent, enhance corporate elegance, productivity. However, it's far currently hampered by way of the hostility, disrespect and discrimination human beings with various historical past encounter within the place of business. Such behavioral attitudes as ascribed to prejudices and biases in the direction of people with varied life-style picks, ethnic and cultural variations, disabilities, and generational gaps. These factors can stifle morale, teamwork, profitability and the beauty of the employer. Consequently, cutting-edge day businesses need to cope with the causes of those troubles to exploit the blessings of WPD. These may be addressed strategies that foster an empowerment lifestyle, construct communiqué and crew spirit with enterprises. These efforts will sell recognition, productivity, and earnings in future firms.

Objectives

- To analyze what are the benefits and drawbacks of diversity prevailing in the society.
- To examine benefits against challenges caused by the different kind of diversity.
- To cognizance on subjects along with race, ethnicity, gender, sexuality, faith, bodily capacity, language, and/or social magnificence with an emphasis on the analysis of fairness.

Discussions

The main motto is to understand what are the benefits and challenges associated with the diversity. The benefits that are carried on by diversity are –

- **Diversity move inventiveness and drive advancement** - Our way of life impacts the manner by which we see the world. Different cultures, background means having different perspective, which will lead in more creativity and will also bring upgradation in society whereas in companies. Assorted variety of idea has been appeared to breed inventiveness and drive advancement, tackling issues with energising ways.

- **Provides a good understanding of Local Market makes business more competitive** – Diversity supports the thinking ability of a person and make the local market easier to understand which can provide an important extremity for venturing into new business. It is possible because by diversity we get to know local laws, guidelines, and traditions, just as the focused scene and can assist a business with thriving. Also, nearby associations, local language abilities, and social comprehension can support worldwide business advancement exponentially. If there will be upgradation in businesses our society will get more modified and we will get a newer version of diversity but in a positive way.
- **It leads to higher quality, Targeted Marketing** More diversity means more advancement in thinking and innovation that leads to higher quality.It provides a base to understand the cultural sensitivity, insight of the local market so as to achieve higher quality then whether it is a good or service.
- **A different aptitudes base enables an association to offer a more extensive and progressively versatile scope of items and administrations-** Diversity will provide a new scope to the society for betterment by suggesting new learning, capabilities, skills, improvement in knowledge and by sorting out the problems caused due to differences .A more extensive abilities base will

offer an improved administrations having the scope of flexibility whenever and wherever required.

- **Greater opportunity for growth as an individual and as an organization-** Diversity itself welcomes talent, perception, learning, change in attitude and behaviour, brings out the best personality within an individual and to develop as an embellished human. Hence provides greater opportunity for upgradation of individual in his or her own forte and by developing themself they will serve the society for further development.

The challenges associated with diversity are-

- **Individual from certain societies might be less inclined to give their voices a chance to be heard-** The nearness of assorted mental aptitude alone isn't sufficient. It's likewise basic to make an open and comprehensive working environment condition, so all individuals feel engaged to contribute. This can be especially trying for associates from gracious or respectful societies. For instance Asian people may feel uncomfortable with the language of China while understanding their language or sharing their ideas.
- **Mix crosswise over multicultural groups can be troublesome even with preference or negative social generalizations -** Managing people of different perception and background is a much more difficult. Same happens when we use to consider too many opinions. Multicultural groups may get confused while selecting the best out of those opinions and if the best one is also selected they will consider it as preference of that particular group. These negative social generalizations can be truly unfavorable to organization assurance and influence profitability.
- **Communication can be misjudged or hard to comprehend crosswise over dialects and societies-**

While quality interpretations are key areas for viable advertising, there can likewise be a genuine danger of correspondence losing all sense of direction in interpretation among multicultural partners. Language boundaries are only one test. Indeed, even in an office where everybody communicates in English, appreciating a scope of accents, or understanding a local speaker's utilization of phrases, can be troublesome.

- **Understandings of expert etiquettes** - People from various societies can likewise carry with them diverse work environment mentalities, qualities, practices, and behavior. While these can be improving and even useful in an assorted proficient condition, they can likewise cause mistaken assumptions or sick sentiments between other individuals.
- **Different Working style can lead to conflict**- Due to differentiated cultures, attitudes, perceptions, skills, qualities the working style of each and every individual is different from another one which may not be liked by the other person of the same competency and area which gives rise to certain conditions in which one of them is Conflict.
- **Regarding and Accepting the Differences of Others-** A specific issue that emerges in work environments is managing social contrasts. Some portion of this may originate from an absence of comprehension or regard. However they are working or living together at some extent they may have differences while regarding or accepting each other's background and tradition.
- **Maintaining Equality-** India is a democratic country where each and every individual has their own rights and responsibilities but instead of it maintaining equality in the laws, treatment with the individual has remained lack somewhere. Sometimes individuals may feel unfairness with

the decisions taken by the competent authority this is because of diversity in their mentalities and aptitudes or may the authority can do the unjust with the individual due to cultural differences or if he / she is much orthodox in nature. In both the cases it becomes very difficult to resolve the conflict rose or to maintain equality.

Implications

Diversity in itself is complex and understanding it is difficult but not impossible. The main reason of destructed comradeship is giving more attention to diversity in sex, religion, race, aptitudes, etc. Assorted variety in the public eye exists on a wide range of levels and can profoundly affect human brain science. These previously mentioned positive and negative effects demonstrate that the effect of assorted variety on social union is blended; the appropriate response relies upon the component of coordination. The two restricting perspectives on the social effect of assorted variety are not conflicting. Or maybe, they catch various parts of the real world. Assorted variety in the work environment is undeniably more unpredictable than applying great and terrible marks and regularly has both positive and negative impacts. A potential advantage is an expansion in imagination however potential difficulties incorporate an expansion in clashes and a breakdown in correspondence.

Issues frequently emerge when organizations limit their viewpoints of assorted variety to the customary statistic contrasts of sex, race, and nationality. Associations should represent other significant statistic contrasts (e.g., incapacity, religion, sexual direction), social/mental contrasts (e.g., correspondence style), and business-related contrasts (e.g., subject matters, residency) that can be outfit to catch better approaches for deduction and critical thinking that can profit the associations. By understanding all the pros and cons we can redress more probable ideas to resolve the problems rose by diversity and can endorse a good sense of brotherhood in the society.

Conclusion

This study is geared towards addressing the positive and negative impacts of diversity on society and analyzes it in a complete sense. Multiculturalism can enable people to comprehend their very own social inclinations and preferences. Diversity has more negative influences on the society because dealing with the diversity it is a challenge and aforesaid challenges affects the society more. Different societies have various thoughts regarding what they need from their specialists, and these discoveries help the experts to adjust their style to be increasingly successful in various social settings. The discoveries can enable worldwide pioneers to impart all the more successfully crosswise over social and geographic limits but not completely as because the same may not be liked by the other one or be according to the other one. So according to the study it is concluded that "diversity in the society prompting change" is a challenge for the society to deal with.

REFERENCES

1. Llopis, Glenn. (2013). "Diversity Management Is the Key to Growth: make it authentic" *Forbes magazine*.
2. Katie, R. (2019). *Benefits and challenges of cultural diversity in the workplace*. Retrieved from.www.hult.edu/blog/benefits-challenges-cultural-diversity-workplace/.
3. Steven, V. (2010). *Diversity, social interaction and solidarity*. Retrieved from www.mpg.de/19440/ Diversity_interaction_solidarity.
4. Bendl, R.; Bleijenbergh, I.; Henttonen, E. & Mills Albert J. (2015). *Handbook of Diversity in Organizations*, Oxford University Press, DOI: 10.13140/2.1.3542.0968.
5. **Jeffrey, G. R. (2010).** *Social impact of diversity: Potentials and challenges in Canada*. **University of Toronto** Guest Contributor.
6. Gupta, Y. (2011). Understanding the Importance of Diversity. *Bloomberg Business Week*.

18

Impact and Challenges of Workforce Diversity in Corporate Hospitals and Healthcare Institutions at Kolkata, West Bengal

Smita Chakraborty

ABSTRACT

One of the complex management phenomena in organizations, in today's world is Workforce Diversity. It is a concept to bring variety of people from various places, caste and creed together under one roof for professional purpose. It acts as a tool to bring about effectiveness, cultivate success and provide equal opportunities within the organization. It is an important issue in both the private and government organizations. The increase in population, mobility, recognized human rights resulted in improved political and economic systems, which in turn resulted in workforce diversity. Diversity brings along heterogeneity which needs to be nurtured and appreciated by means of increasing effectiveness within the company. Thus, it is considered as one of the main challenges for Human Resource Management in modern organizations. Despite its strategic importance, majority of models in this field considers workforce as homogenous and generic and does not take into account the cultural differences among employees.

Introduction

Diversity management intends to create and maintain a positive work environment where the similarities and differences of individuals are valued, so that all can reach their potential and maximize their contributions to an organization's strategic goals and objectives. It ensures that all employees have the opportunity to maximize their potential and enhance their self-development and their contribution to the organization. It recognizes that people from different backgrounds can bring fresh ideas and perceptions, which can make the way work is done more efficient and make products and services better. Managing diversity successfully will help organizations to nurture creativity and innovation and thereby to tap hidden capacity for growth and improved competitiveness. The aim of this study is to provide a systematic literature review on diversity among employees in strategic human resource management (SHRM) and to identify the limitations, challenges and unresolved issues of this concept.

Review of Literature

Workforce Diversity is broadly defined as a planned and systematic commitment of the organizations to recruit and promote a heterogeneous mix of employees in the organization. Diversity Management techniques and theories have been developed and supported by training specialists, consultants, executives and academicians (Saji, 2004)[1] . It leads to employee co-existence from various socio cultural backgrounds and also includes cultural factors like gender, race, color, age, ethnicity, physical ability, national origin, disability, religion, sexual orientation, education, values, beliefs, language lifestyle, physical appearances and economic status (Wentling& Rivas, 2000)[2]. It creates an environment where each and every employee can pursue his or her career without being inhibited by race, gender, religion and other factors that are barriers to their performances (Bryan, 1999)[3]. It thus increases organizational effectiveness and helps to attract the best employees to work with (Carrell& Mann et al., 2006)[4]. At present diversity is an important issue in all sectors including legal, political and corporate and managingthis workforce diversity has become the most important and challenging task of modern organizations (Reilly & Williams, 1998)[5]. It promotes a unique and creative approach for solving problems in the workplace. It creates innovation and creativity which in turn leads to effective organizational goals (Allen et al., 2007)[6]. A diverse work-force provides better output as it helps better understanding of customer needs (Wentling& Rivas, 2000)[7]. For an organization to develop and prosper in the society as a whole, creating and managing a diverse workforce should be seen as a social responsibility (Muller, 1998)[8]. With increase in globalization, organizations will be benefited by diversity to enter the international arena (Cascio, 2000)[9]. It also enriches the human capital in the organization and minimizes cloning which in the long run promotes innovative ideas and abilities, scope and competitive performance. On the other hand, it is also important to understand that diversity along with its benefits and advantages brings with it various challenges as the road to diversity is not very smooth. Not only energy, skills and a considerable amount of time is needed to maintain a diverse workplace (Farrer, 2004)[10], it also consists of organizational challenges like trust, commitment, work-life balance, workplace authority, innovative work ethics, proper firm structure (McCuiston et al., 2004)[11], perceived discrimination, conflicts and costs to training which resulted from diversity promotional programs (White, 1999)[12].

Objectives

- To find out whether the concept of work-force diversity is applicable or not in corporate hospitals and healthcare institutions of Kolkata, West Bengal.
- To study the extent of acceptability of work-force diversity incorporate hospitals and healthcare

institutions in Kolkata, West Bengal.

- To study the impact that work-force diversity will have on the employee performance in corporate hospitals and healthcare institutions of Kolkata, West Bengal.
- To find out ways to overcome challenges of work-force diversity in the corporate hospital sectors of Kolkata, West Bengal.

Discussion

The concept of diversity includes acceptance and respect as each individual is unique and has differences. Dimensions of differences can be of race, ethnicity, gender, sexual orientation, socio-economic status, age, physical abilities, religious beliefs, political beliefs, or other ideologies. The exploration of these dissimilarities should be in a safe and positive environment. It is about understanding each other and embracing and recognizing the rich dimensions of diversity within each individual. Diversity is a set of conscious practice which involves understanding and appreciating inter-dependence of humanity, culture and natural environment. It involves practicing mutual respect of individual in terms of quality and experiences. It is also a way of recognizing the fact that personal, cultural, and organizational discrimination creates and sustains privileges for some, whereas it creates disadvantages for others. Diversity involves not only how people perceive themselves but also how they perceive others and those perceptions affect their interactions as well. For employees to function effectively as an organization, human resource professionals need to deal effectively with issues such as communication, adaptability, and changes. Diversity management is a process which is intended to create and maintain a positive work environment where the similarities and differences of individuals are valued, so that all can reach their potential and maximize their contributions to an organization's strategic goals and objectives. Thus, this study aims to find out the impact and the challenges of workforce diversity in healthcare sector in Kolkata, West Bengal. The goal of this research is to benefit the employees and the society and bring out productive output of the organization.

Implications

Hospital and Healthcare Industries is one of the oldest and the most established industries in recent times. It has a long history of serving a huge population and hiring employees from all demographic region. This sector is spread out throughout the national and international arena of the globe. Thus, having a diverse work-force concept within the organizations is essential. It adds value by strategic usage means. This paper critically analyses the impact of workforce diversity on the productivity of the organizations and the challenges of workforce diversity concept within the corporate healthcare sectors of Kolkata, West Bengal.

Conclusion

In today's globalization environment, Workforce Diversity has become an important concept in the organizational human resource profile. Workforce nowadays has lost its homogeneity and shifted to heterogeneity. This improves employee morale, corporate culture, increases employee retention, promotes better employee recruitment, builds a more qualified healthcare team, decreases complaints and inter-personal clashes, increases employee productivity and helps to bring about innovative ideas. This diversity is viewed as a positive force for employees job performance. Furthermore, Workforce Diversity is closely related to Human Resource Management in organizations to attract and recruit the most talented people from a pool of workforce. This study firstly aims to help the society as common people will be willing to work in healthcare organization which has diversity in its workforce. It will also find out whether the concept of diverse work-force is acceptable in the corporate hospitals or not and how much it is affecting the employee performance of the corporate hospitals and healthcare institutions of Kolkata, West Bengal.

REFERENCES

1. Saji, B. (2004). Workforce Diversity, Temporal Dimensions and Team Performance, Cross Cultural Management. *An International Journal*. 11(4). p.p: 40-59.
2. Wrentling, M & Rivas, N. (2001). Current Status of Diversity Initiatives in Selected Multinational Corporations. *Human Resource Development Quarterly*. 11(1). p.p :35-60.
3. Bryan, H. (1999). The Diversity Imperative: Executive Excellence. p.p :6.
4. Carrell, M & Mann, E et al., (2006). Defining Workforce Diversity Programs and Practices in Organizations : A Longitudinal Study. *Labor Law Journal*. 57(1). p.p :1-5.
5. Williams, K & Reilly, C. (1998). Demography and Diversity in Organizations. *OrganizatialBehaviour*. 2. p.p: 77-140.
6. Allen, R. & Wheatley, K. et al., (2007). Perceived Diversity and Organizational Performance. *Journal Employee Relations*. 30(1). p.p: 20-33.
7. Wentling, R & Rivas, N. (2000). Current Status of Diversity initiatives in seleted multinational corporations. *Human Resource Development Quarterly*. 11(1). p.p: 35-60.
8. Muller, H. (1998). Integrating Workforce Diversity into the Business School Curriculum: An Experiment. *Journal of Management Education*. 22(2). p.p: 122-148.
9. Cascio, W. (2000). Managing a Virtual Workplace. *Academy of Management Executive*.14(3). p.p: 81-90.
10. Farrer, J. (2004). A Practical Approach to Diversity. *Industrial and Commercial Training Edition*. 36(4). p.p: 175-177.
11. McCuiston, V. & Wooldridge, B et al., (2004). Leading the Diverse Workforce: Profit, Prospects and Progress. *Leadership and Organizational Journal*. 25(1). p.p: 73-92.
12. White, R. (1999). Managing the Diverse Organization: The Imperative for a new Multicultural Paradigm. *Journal of Public Administration and Management*. 4(4). p.p: 53-69.

19

Women in Work: Gender Diversity and Inequality in an Organization

Abanti Aich

ABSTRACT

Women's participation has been comparatively increasing and developing in an organization. Women are equality participating in the workplace just like men. Often women are not given first priority comparing to man. Sometimes in many areas women security is also lacking in their workplace. In an organization there are some odd issues faced by women, but many of them overcome the obstacles and build their career. The women play an important role in an organization in the process of completion of many tasks and duties. Some of them compel to take break in the workplace due to unavoidable factors and to manage the work and life balance.

Introduction

Some issues are created due to sudden shift bases work in organization for particular women. Many women also find difficulties for the time of maternity leave. They cannot owe the proper facilities and are underestimated by the organization. Women also experience lot of differentiation in their work area and also disturbed by their colleague and also suffer sociological interruption in organization. Gender diversity and inequality is another complex phenomenon in the workplace. These cause the generation of high level of stress among the women at organization. All these things also affect their personal life. The growing inequality must absorbed and new employment should be designed in a new way which restructures the organizational infrastructure so that when people start working then the organizational dimension may metamorphose. Gender diversity is one of the common events in society and organization. Gender diversity is representation of people of different genders. Employees of both genders should be trained about the advantages of gender equality and also built up the awareness about gender equality.

Review of Literature

Diversity means the mixture of imputations in organization that shows how people feel, think and behave at work and their work performance, progress, acceptance of satisfaction in their organization (Thomas & Bendick, 2013). Gender inequality is complex phenomenon in organization (Stamarski & Son Hong, 2015). Sometimes women feel uneasy in their organization due to the multiple forms of inequalities present in their workplace (Abrams, 1991). Women are trying to prove them self in many areas. Women are the equal participant just like man (Shruthi & Ramu, 2018) . Women faces many problem in organization but some of them overcome these obstacles and make their carrier successful (Patwardhan, et al., 2016). Women possess them self by overcoming all the obstacles. This is caused by the support and encouragement from their friends and family members. This will encourage women to develop and fulfill their goals (Garg & Agarwal, 2017). There are many social obstacles. Many women are sexually harassed by their co-workers (Hays & Morrow, 2013). Social and organization culture become hurdle for women's development in their organization (Catalyst, 2003). Some issues are created due to the shifting work in organization.

The gender diversity and inequality cause very high level of tension among the women in the organization that effect personal life very badly (Stamarski & Son-Hong, 2015). Being a member of the same organization the women are paid less compared to men for the same profession and same experience (Jacobs, 1992). Married women work force is being defeated because of the employment obstruction. Sometime organizer is unwilling to recruit married women especially who are mothers (Adler, 1993). Many women find out difficulties in the time of maternity leave period. In this situation the women are underrated by the other employs of organization (Kawachi, et al., 1999). Despite lot of problems number of women is increasing in organizations. Women not only have engaged in their organization they also have reached higher standard and expanded their position in organization (Wilson-Kovacs, et al., 2006).

Objectives

The main objective of this article is identifying the factors cause women diversity and inequality in organization. Some predictors were marked out as factors which cause women diversity and inequality in organization. They include pay inequality, sexual harassment, sudden change in duty shift, work- life conflict, difficulties in the time of maternity period. This study also determines the relationship between the gender diversity and women inequality in organization and finds out the reason of women inequality an organization along with the way to solve the inequality and diversity problem in organization. This study also identifies the relationship of organizational culture towards the women inequality in organization.

Framework of the Study

From the above study, framework is exhibited and proposed to examine the factors which cause women inequality in organization.

Fig 1. Proposed conceptual framework for the study

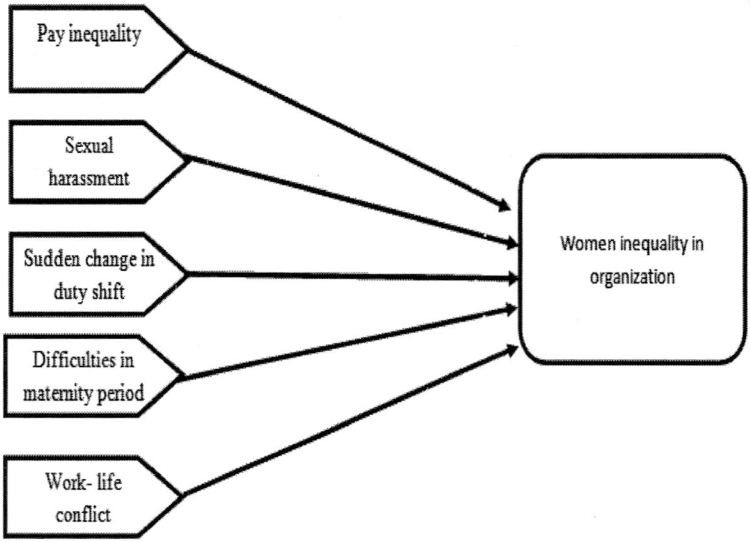

Discussion

The present study dissected the gender inequality of women in organization and explained that the women face many problems at their workplace and also personal life several parameters are identified associated with the this as congeniality in their organization, culture and atmosphere in workplace and the difficulties which has faced by women in their organization. It also highlighted difficulties that the women faces in their organization also affect their personal life. This study also prospects the way, how the women employees think and feel at their organization. It also uncovered the women's experience and opinion at their organization and what kind of change occurs in their life after joining as an employee in organization.

Implications

Gender inequality and gender diversity is complex phenomenon. It directly or indirectly affects the time of hiring, promotion, pay and training of women employees.

Most organizations have their own aspects. As a result gender inequality and gender diversity has become an important issue for working women in organization. This study shows that it is indeed a big challenge for women to overcome it and to prove themselves in their workplace. In this study, the most negatives of diversity and inequality were noticed and displayed the gender inequality and gender diversity. This study focuses on the obstacles of women employees in their organization which shows that, the difference of gender inequality and gender diversity between men and women in organization is remarkably alarming. This study-result showed that many of them overcame those obstacles and reached higher standards and position in organization to build a good carrier prospective.

Conclusion

The women diversity and inequality is a reflection of a changing universe. It is a global phenomenon. This study accomplish that women face many problem and issues in organization that effect not only their workplace but also their personal life. This article focuses on women's independent effect at organization as well as their personal life. This study has experience of women and their opinion on their organization atmosphere. Although there are many difficulties in organization, the women employees still overcome those obstacles and lead a successful life in their respective field. Successful women stand as a role model of inspiration and motivation for many women who fell depressed.

REFERENCES

1. Thomas, H. & Bendick, M. (2013). Professionalizing Diversity and Inclusion Practice: Should Voluntary Standards Be the Chicken or the Egg? *Industrial and Organizational Psychology*. 6(3). Pp. 193-205. DOI: 10.1111/iops.12033.
2. Stamarski, CS. & Son Hong, LS. (2015). Gender inequalities in the workplace: the effects of organizational structures,

processes, practices, and decision makers' sexism. *Frontiers in psychology*.6:1400. DOI: 10.3389/fpsyg.2015.01400.

3. Abrams, K. (1991). Social Construction, Roving Biologism, and Reasonable Women: A Response to Professor Epstein. *DePaul Law Review*.41. Pp-1C21-1040.
4. Patwardhan,V., Maya, S & Joshi, H.G. (2016). Barriers To Career Advancement Of Women. *International Journal of Remote Sensing*.Vol.6 (6).Pp.248-253.
5. Garg, S. & Dr. Agarwal, P. (2017). Problems and Prospects of Woman Entrepreneurship – A Review of Literature. *IOSR Journal of Business and Management*. 19(1). PP 55-60. e-ISSN: 2278-487, p-ISSN: 2319-7668.
6. Shruthi, S. & Ramu, M. (2018). A study on the women at workplace with special reference to the geographically mobile qualified and liberated as a global phenomenon. *International Journal of Pure and Applied Mathematics*. 120 (5). pp. 595-612. ISSN: 1314-3395.
7. Hays, N & Morrow, K. (2013). Gender Discrimination At Workplace. © 2013 Hays Morrow. Pp.4-25.
8. Catalyst. (2003). Report-Women in US Corporate Leadership. Catalyst .New York.
9. Stamarski, CS. & Son Hong, LS. (2015). Gender inequalities in the workplace: the effects of organizational structures, processes, practices, and decision makers' sexism. *Frontiers in psychology*.6:1400. DOI: 10.3389/fpsyg.2015.01400.
10. Jacobs, J. A. (1992). Women's entry into management: Trends in earnings, authority, and values among salaried managers. *Administrative Science Quarterly*. 37(2).pp-282-301.
11. Adler,N.J. (1993) An International Perspective on the Barriers to the Advancement of Women Managers. *Applied Psychology: An International Review*. 42(4). pp- 289-300.
12. Kawachi, I.et .al. (1999) Women's status and the health of women and men: a view from the States. *Social Science & Medicine* .48(1). Pp: 21-32.
13. Wilson-Kovacs, D.M. et al. (2006) "The glass cliff: women's career paths in the UK private IT sector", *Equal Opportunities International*, 25 (8). pp.674-687.

20

A Study on Cloud based Inventory Control Management in Urban Hospital of West Bengal

Swatee Biswas

ABSTRACT

One of the reasons behind the smooth functioning of hospitals is its inventory. Hospital inventory includes commonly used drugs, injections, surgical equipments and medical related stocks. Thus a proper management is required for the inventory control. In the era of modernization, companies are investing on technologies to gain a competitive advantage. Inventory management system is an old concept in many retail sectors but hospitals of healthcare sector has introduced it recently. Cloud Computing is the latest software that provide various kind of solutions. It is a cost effective method that eases real time data collection, data storage and data exchange between health care organizations. This study focuses on amalgamation of inventory management system and Cloud Computing to understand the benefit and advantage that the hospital sectors gains from it. This study is completely done on the basis of secondary data, which is collected from various articles and journals.

Keywords: *Cloud Computing, inventory management system, advantages, modernization*

Introduction

Inventory control management is a logical integration between material in stock and material demanded for. It is the process to maintain a balanced supply chain where procurement and distribution in right quantity at right time on right place is anticipated (Rosetti,2008). The concept of inventory management is quite popular in retail market. But this concept is given a less value in healthcare sector. With the tide of modernization, inventory control management is introduced in recent studies, which has witnessed many benefits. Study has approximately found that proper inventory management system has reduced the total costs which include the capital cost, storage cost and risk costs. It has been easier with the latest technology to maintain the control over inventory management system in hospital. Every department is responsible for gaining satisfaction of patient or patient party. Likewise, inventory system within the hospital may not be directly responsible but it is responsible indirectly. Hospital inventory must maintain a good stock of life saving medicines, injections, and disposable surgical items like syringe, masks, gloves and many more. This study basically focuses on the importance of installation of cloud based inventory management system in hospitals.

Literature Review

Inventory management is one of the oldest and well acceptable concepts that are used since many years in retail sector. When it comes to healthcare sector, inventory management system is one of the most complicated in comparison with other sectors. Unlike any other sector inventory system under this sector deals with patient needs (Noorfa et al., 2009). Sometimes the unpredictable situational demand is responsible for complexity in inventory management system in healthcare sector (Vikram et al., 2012). Some activities in health care sector like procurement, transportation, Information and

Communication system (ICT) management, inventory monitoring etc are followed like in any other organizations (Xiong et al., 2007). A Cloud based Inventory Management System is the new development that has been introduced. However proper configuration is needed before shifting from traditional inventory management system to the new Cloud based inventory management system. One of the prior tasks is to understand all the factors to assure the implementation of Cloud based technology in inventory management system (Schramm et al., 2010). There are many activities where Cloud Computing has stepped in. Some of the activities are logistics, procurement and sourcing, planning and forecasting etc. These activities have given remarkable results on implementation of Cloud based concept in inventory control (Toka et al., 2013). This paper more initiates that benefits like cost-efficiency, visibility, flexibility etc gives competitive advantage in hospitals.

Execution of Cloud Computing in Inventory Management System

Planning and Forecasting

The main aim of the hospital is to increase the satisfaction level of patients. Thus, it is important to have coordination between inventory management system and its partner to keep an eye on the things demanded. Planning and Forecasting is a continuous process that can be done using cloud-based software. This result in more accurate forecasts regarding unavailability of the equipments and other stuffs required in hospitals. This process of continuous monitoring will help in reducing the Bullwhip effect in different stages of inventory management system (Lee et al., 1997). Cloud also provide a combination of electronic data interchange and forecast execution application in a single platform for all the inventory management system partners to well understand the enquiries and demand at real time (Pires & Camarge, 2010).

Logistics

A continuous monitoring on the inventory management system reduces the extra cost and leads to save annual freight cost for the organization. There are different kinds of medicines or medical equipments like disposable surgical items that need to be carried carefully. So right things on right place at right time in right condition is ensured which is the primary objective of logistics and the cloud can make it easier, more efficient and less costly.

Service and Spare Parts Management

Cloud Computing provides a platform to the sector where forward and reverse logistics can be monitored (Guid et. al., 2003). Radio frequency identification is a technology that helps in tracking location of inventory. All this detail are then transmitted to computer application. With these it is easy to track the route and any misconduct will be captured wisely. This helps to maintain the return policy and warranty validation (Schramm et al., 2010)

Sourcing and Procurement

Healthcare sector are rapidly growing, thus demand are also increasing with it. The platform of Cloud helps to maintain the huge data related to different suppliers. It moreover helps in tracking the benefits obtained from different sources, a continuous monitoring over the specified demand and its fulfillment with time helps to maintain a balance in inventory management system (Toka et al., 2013).

Benefits

Cost Efficiency

Cloud based Technology has provided with many benefits that gives a benefit of cost efficiency in the various field of hospitals. Initially unlike any other software's (namely ERP), Cloud-based system does not claim the charges for different functions like charges on software, charges on computer ownership, etc. Thus it reduces the initial hardware and software charges (Peiser, 2018) and just makes a payment for first time activation and then according to the uses. Moreover maintenance of data requires a huge cost but with Cloud Computing the headache of maintaining is optimal (Peiser, 2018).

Simplification

Inventory system includes huge work process in different stages and through Cloud Computing every stage of inventory system is accessible on a single platform. It eliminates the hurdles and complications related to inconvenience of sharing information with the concerned authority and provide easiest possible solutions in one shared platform (Chen & Ma Yan 2011). Certain security concern is there for independent access to the information. Thus open access is not given to everyone but members can be added at any point of time with the login credentials (Pires & Camargo, 2010).

Visibility

Visibility is one of the key features of Cloud Computing over inventory management system since it provides a tracking facility at real time. It is also known as "Visual Warehouse for the available items". This helps the organization to make faster decisions and strategy. It also helps in forecasting future procurements (Gtnexus, 2009). Unexpected deviation can be overcome with this feature of Cloud Computing.

Flexibility

Cloud based inventory management system made employees more flexible to complete the task in and out of the workplace. It also allows the employees to access or update inventory data from any device and location in real-time. This eliminates manual data transmission delays.

Scalability

Scalability is one of the most valuable features of Cloud Computing. To meet the demand there is no need to purchase new hardware or storage space. This is done by Cloud Service Provider. It allows rapid adjustment according to variations. It allows the inventory control management to upscale and down scale the storage to accommodate their needs.

Sustainability

A large percentage of energy costs can be saved by switching to cloud facility. Cloud reduces carbon emissions through minimized energy requirements. According to (Abood, et al., 2010) there is a significant decrease in CO_2 emission per user using cloud based platform. However many doubts that saving energy does not always mean reducing Greenhouse gas emissions. Despite all this to be environmentally sustainable this Cloud Computing centers should be located in places from where it can draw a large amount of power from renewable sources of energy and Google has been one of the major investor in Renewable and it is using that energy to power its own business. So by locating the cloud in areas that source renewable power, Cloud Computing can save millions of dollars in energy cost and can reduce carbon emissions significantly.

Implications

A large number of hospitals in urban West Bengal still facing serious problem with the practice of its distribution process and inventory management. Collection of data and inventory checking are still conducted in manual way which takes a lot of time and result in errors due to miscalculation. This study will mainly focus in improving inventory management system using cloud based services.

As a large amount of money is spent on purchasing medical material and supplies so it requires a significant system to manage inventory in hospitals. This study will help to reduce unnecessary purchases as it will help in transferring quickly the idle inventory from one place to another place where it is needed. This cloud based system can help in tracking accurately the medical inventory such as supply stock levels, the medication which is about to expire and where the equipment is. This will limit the waste of time. The mental pressure on the administrators will reduce and the staffs can spend more time on patient care which is one of the main agenda of this study.

Cloud based system will improve the accuracy by providing updated inventory information in real time which will prevent inventory theft and thereby reduce the cost significantly.

The control of disease starts with inventory management. By proper tracking of surgical instruments, it can prevent the use of infected instruments with other patients.

The hospitals usually make contracts with the product distributors and manufacturers so that they can obtain it at lower costs. This automated inventory management system will eliminate the risk of stock out and prevent from forceful buy of products outside the contractual terms at higher price.

Conclusion

This study has highlighted the importance of inventory in hospitals. For smooth functioning the hospital cannot overlook the competitive advantage that is concerned with inventory management system. Installation of Cloud Computing boosts up the flow of inventory management system. It is found that amalgamation of Cloud and inventory management system give the advantages like cost efficiency, scalability, visibility, flexibility etc. This study sheds light on the factor that acceptance of modern technology will provide them numerous advantages.

REFERENCES

1. Abood, D.; Murdoch, R.; N'Diaye, S.; Albano, D.; Kofmehl, A.; Tung, T. & Whitney, J. (2010). "Cloud computing and sustainability: The environmental benefits of moving to the cloud".*Accenture*. Retrieved from http://www.accenture.com/usen/pages/index.aspx
2. Bhakoo, V.; Singh, P. & Sohal, A. (2012) "Collaborative Management of Inventory in Australian Hospital Supply Chain: Practices and Issues", *Emerald Group Publishing Limited*.
3. Chen, J. & Ma Yan, W. (2011) "The research of supply chain information collaboration based on cloud computing" *Procedia Environmental Sciences*, 10(A), 875-880.
4. Guide, V.; Harrison, T. & Van Wassenhove, L. (2003). The challenge of closed-loop supply chains. Interfaces: *The INFORMS Journal of Operations Research*, 33(6), 3–6.
5. Lee, H.; Padmanabhan, V. & Whang, S. (1997). Information distortion in a supply chain: The bullwhip effect. *Management Science*, 43(4), 546–558. doi:10.1287/mnsc.43.4.546.
6. Mustaffa, N. & Potter, A., (2009) "Healthcare Supply Chain Management in Malaysia: a case study", *Emerald Group Publishing, Supply Chain Management: an International Journal*, 14(3), pp. 234-243.
7. Nexus, G. T. (2009). Visibility in the import supply chain. GT Nexus Inc. Retrieved from http://www.gtnexus.com/
8. Pires, S. & Camargo, J. B. (2010). "Using cloud computing to integrate processes in the supply chain". *In Proceedings of the POMS 21st Annual Conference*. Vancouver, Canada: POMS
9. Rosetti (2008). "Inventory Management Issues in Healthcare Supply Chain", *University of Arkansas*, USA.
10. Schramm, T.; Wright, J.; Seng, D. & Jones, D. (2010)."Six questions every supply chain executive should ask about cloud computing". *Accenture*. Retrieved from http://www.accenture.com/usen/pages/index.aspx
11. Toka, A.; Aivazidou, E.; Antoniou, A. & Darginis, K. A. (2013) "Cloud Computing in Supply Chain Management: An Overview". DOI: 10.13140/2.1.2717.2800.
12. Xiong, Z. & Shaligram, P. (2007) "Logistics Innovation Process Revisited: insight from a hospital case study", *International Journal of Physical Distribution and Management*, 41(6), pp. 577-600.

21

Recent Trends in Recruitment in Modern Management

Manali Basu

ABSTRACT

Being the most important aspect of business, recruitment is always on priority list of any of the organization. Technology is changing, and organizations are accepting changes and trying to make the recruitment process more effective than ever before. Presently, there are going to be some new developments in the recruitment space worldwide, as each year brings with it a host of exciting possibilities. This paper examines the scenario of the recruitment and recent trend of recruitment in modern management.

Introduction

Recruitment is the process of filling up of vacancy in an organization. It can easily be considered to be one of the most critical functions of an organization. As we know business environment becomes more competitive. It is really very tough to find out the right people with the right skills for the right tasks. To make a successful hiring decision is one of the important parts of the management. Talent management always refers the process of recruiting, hiring, retaining right fit, top performance for the organization.

Objectives

- To know new recruitment trend.
- To know the importance of implementing new recruitment trend.
- To know present scenario of recruitment globally.

Research Methodology

The research study is based on secondary data. I have collected all information from various published research, articles, books, reports etc. and these are from online.

Recent Trend in Recruitment

For the organization, we all know that turnover at all level is costly and can destroy any chances for making a profit. Not only that but also organizations transform organization into a talent management. Efficient employee always they will try to eliminate turnover and reach their goal. Many organizations hire business trainers and consultant. They develop new strategies and tactics to implement better plan to secure future goal. If I say about the recent trend of recruitment in modern management, Recruitment Marketing currently introduced as a consequences of the present situation in labour market. The main objective of the Recruitment Marketing is to follow the latest trend in the market and offer solution to overcome the tough situation.Inbound Marketingis another strategy to attract, convert and engage candidate. If organization is looking for long term solution to advance recruiting and hiring strategy, Inbound Recruitment organization should adopt.Employee Brandingideas are essential for building a strong and attractive employer brand, not only attract employee but also the struggle to retain employee.In Candidate Experience candidate who had a positive candidate experience in organization's recruiting process, will more likely accept their job offer and reapply in future and refer others to company.In Talent Pool recruiter creates data base, where they keep all their top candidates thathas applied for the job and also sourced and referred. Talent pools make not only candidates that have applied for jobs, but also sourced, referred candidates that have willingly joined pool in an inbound way.Candidate Relationship Management manages and improves relationship with current and potential future of job candidates.Social Recruitingis a way through this; you can attract potential candidates (Examples, Facebook, Twitter, websites, Blogsetc.).GDPR (General Data Protection Regulation) introduced on 25th May 2018, one of the most recent trend in recruitment. It controls the personal data or information which means it will completely change the way recruiting operates in 2019.Data Driven Recruiting and HR analytic based on planning and decision making. It always give focuses on which part of your hiring strategy work well and also focuses on cost to hiring, time to hiring and qualityof hiring.Employee Referralis productive way of hiring. May research has proven that referred employees take shortest to hire and on board and require way less money.Talent Sourcing is also one of the important sources of recruitment now a day.Collaborative Hiring is a method where, HR department along with other department collectively work together to hire potential employee. It has chosen as top 15 recruitment trend for 2019.Structured Interview, now a days is very popular, clear and effective way.Strategic Alignment is very important for each and every company. Without talent or effective people company can't grow. So, recruitment should be more strategic to fulfil future goal.

Overview of Recruitment in world's most reputable companies

There are various types of successful business in this world. They improve the lives of their consumers. They work with brilliant and inspiring business leaders and also with their talented employee. This is the main source of their success. Before hire anyone, successful organization always focuses on good planning. Not only that but also they are flexible with their good organizational skills.The Walt Disney, commonly known as Disney, founded on October 16, 1923 by brothers Walt and Roy o. Disney. It is one of the most reputed companies in this world. They always look at a resume a lots of time also they check if the person has their hair combed or the right tie on.They receive application (cover letter, CV). Next level they arrange assessment day, included four main elements-i) Group activity, ii) Office tour iii) Individual excel test iv) Individual interview. Candidates are liable to be asked questions including; what are strengths and weakness, what is your biggest achievements etc.Actually they want know about their candidates give them a true reflection of the company and creates a detailed job specification.Microsoft, also another reputed company, founded by Paul Allen and Bill Gates on April 4, 1975. Conduct 4 to 5 rounds to select fresher. They arrange online round, onsite round, Technical cum HR round. Sony is one of the leading manufacturers of electronic products for the consumer and professional market, conduct recruitment process in different way. They conduct recruitment process every year, consists of three rounds-Written exam, Technical interview, HR interview.On the other hand, Netflix, conduct a very modern process in recruitment, first phase of the recruitment they most use network and try to expand them, this is called sourcing candidates. Next phase they arrange Coffee Dates, it shows that employee is professional or not, punctual or not and so many things. The last phase are interviewing candidates and closing job contracts.In terms of recruitment trends, 2019 will bring a fresh set of recruitment trend that will significantly impact recruiting process. Already, reputed companies have started to implement. If we compare also with the last few years ago the total recruitment process has changed and candidates now have far more power during the job search.

Findings

- Recruiters need to give effort to persuade passive candidates.
- Proper research is very important to get fruitful results in recruitment.
- Recruiters should give more attention on candidates, what motivate them and makes them happy in their job.
- Long time to hire sometimes it may create shortage of qualified candidates.
- Coordination with employee is very important; recruiters should pass proper information about interview.
- Recruiters should maintain fair recruitment process.
- Recruiters should create an efficient recruiting process.

Conclusion

In spite of all problems recruitment is very vital part of the organization. Proper recruitment method always helpful and increase the productivity and profitability of the company. But, there are many areas where need a careful attention. So, there is a need of modern developed technology in organization for a successful recruitment. Attention should be paid for the improvement of the quality in the organization.

REFERENCES

1. HRM Journal, (vol.18, issue 3, Page-257-274)
2. Journal of Entrepreneurship & organization management, omicsonline.org.
3. IOSR Journal of Business & Management (vol.15, Issue 5, Jan 2014, www.iosrjournals.org)

4. www.linkedin.com
5. www.quora.com
6. www.geeksforgeeks.org/intel
7. www.talentlyft.com
8. www.hrhelpboard.com
9. www.kbic.com
10. www.naukrirms.com
11. www.hrmpractice.com
12. www.academia.edu
13. www.resources.workable.com
14. www.reliableplant.com